The Days Between

The Days Between

Blessings, Poems, and Directions of the Heart
for the Jewish High Holiday Season

ימים שבין לבין

ברכות, שירים וכוונות הלב
לעשרת ימי תשובה

Marcia Falk

BRANDEIS UNIVERSITY PRESS
WALTHAM, MASSACHUSETTS

Brandeis University Press
An imprint of University Press of New England
www.upne.com
© 2014 Marcia Lee Falk
All rights reserved
Manufactured in the United States of America
Designed by April Leidig
Typeset in Garamond, and Days and Nights by Ben Nathan
by Tseng Information Systems, Inc.

University Press of New England is a member of the
Green Press Initiative. The paper used in this book
meets their minimum requirement for recycled paper.

For permission to reproduce any of the material in this
book, contact Permissions, University Press of New England,
One Court Street, Suite 250, Lebanon NH 03766; or visit
www.upne.com

Cover art: "Gilead Apples," Marcia Falk, watercolor pencil.
May the year be sweet as apples dipped in honey
and full as the ripe pomegranate
with blessings.

Library of Congress Cataloging-in-Publication Data
Falk, Marcia, author.
The days between: blessings, poems, and directions of the
heart for the Jewish High Holiday season / Marcia Falk.
pages cm. — (HBI series on Jewish women)
ISBN 978-1-61168-605-0 (cloth : alk. paper) —
ISBN 978-1-61168-606-7 (ebook)
1. High Holidays — Prayers and devotions. 2. High Holidays —
Liturgy — Texts. 3. Judaism — Liturgy — Texts. 4. Judaism —
Prayers and devotions. I. Title.
BM665.F36 2014
296.7'2 — dc23   2014002471

5 4 3 2 1

In memory of Frieda Goldberg Falk
dedicated teacher, lover of Judaism,
feminist foremother

פריידע בת רחל ושמואל יהודה
זיכרונה לברכה

In memory of Abraham Abbey Falk
man of compassion,
lover of justice

אברהם אבא בן שלום דוד והינדע
זיכרונו לברכה

And for their grandson,
Abraham Gilead Falk-Rood

אברהם גילעד

Opening the Heart

At the year's turn,
in the days between,

we step away
from what we know

into the spaces
we cannot yet name.

Slowly the edges
begin to yield,

the hard places
soften,

the gate to forgiveness
opens.

תוכן העניינים

חלק ראשון ❧ ראש השנה

לפני השער:
סעודת ליל ראש השנה

פתיחת הלב

*באנגלית

Contents

*English only

נשליך במצולות ים

חלק שני ⟩ חלון, ציפור, רקיע*

שיר של יום וכוונת הלב
לעשרת ימי תשובה

*באנגלית

We Cast into the Depths of the Sea (*Tashlikh* Ritual)

Two ᴥ Window, Bird, Sky*

Daily Psalms and Directions of the Heart for the Ten Days of Returning

*English only

חלק שלישי ❦ יום הכיפורים

התכנסות:
ליל הכיפורים

Three ❧ Yom Kippur

Gathering In:
Yom Kippur Eve

*English only

מאחרית לראשית

חלק רביעי ☙ כניסה בשערים

חלק חמישי ☙ על "ונתנה תוקף קדושת היום"*

*באנגלית

From End to Beginning

Four ✎ Entering the Gates

Five ✎ Re-visioning *Un'taneh Tókef K'dushat Hayom**

*English only

Introduction
🍃 The Days Between

We measure time in lines — forward and back. We count the years of our lives from zero to the end. We count the days from Rosh Hashanah to Yom Kippur: ten.

But we also measure time in cycles — birthdays and memorial days, monthly and yearly holidays, the weekly return of the Sabbath. Spring and fall, and spring again. And we count cycles not from beginning to end but from beginning to beginning. Season begets season, month begets month, day begets day, without pause. No sooner has a year begun than we start counting the days until the next New Year.

The two kinds of time, linear and cyclical, are always with us, and never more so than during the High Holiday season, when darkness and light intermingle. A year has passed, and we are aware of being a year closer to our death. And yet, we are given a chance to start fresh.

The turning of the year — *t'shuvat hashanah*, as the New Year is sometimes referred to in the Bible* — reminds us that all ends are beginnings and all beginnings can be turn-

---

*2 Samuel 11:1, 1 Kings 20:22, 1 Kings 20:26, 1 Chronicles 20:1, and 2 Chronicles 36:10.

ings. As the year turns and we become aware that the days are growing shorter—or, in the Southern Hemisphere, as we see them begin to lengthen—we turn, deliberately and with deliberation, to confront the great challenges of our lives. Who will live and who will die? asks *Un'taneh Tókef K'dushat Hayom* (We Declare the Utter Sanctity of This Day), a central liturgical passage of Rosh Hashanah and Yom Kippur. When and how will we come to our end? To these questions, we may add: What kind of life will we live in the time we have? Where in our life will we find purpose and meaning?

BETWEEN ROSH HASHANAH AND YOM KIPPUR

We often think of the High Holidays—in Hebrew, *Hayamim Hanora'im*, the Days of Awe—as referring to Rosh Hashanah (the New Year holiday) and Yom Kippur (the Day of Atonement). But it is more accurate, and truer to the spirit of the season, to view the High Holidays as a span of time, a continuous progression that begins at the onset of Rosh Hashanah and concludes at the close of Yom Kippur, the holiest day of the year. Another name for this span is *Aséret Y'mey T'shuvah*, the Ten Days of Turning, or Returning. *T'shuvah*, the keynote word of the High Holidays, derives from the Hebrew word-root *shuv*—"to return, to do again." "Repentance," the English translation of *t'shuvah* that is often found in prayer books, is misleading, for it fails to convey the hopefulness embedded in *shuv*, with its promise of new beginnings and second chances. We might instead think of *t'shuvah* as turning the heart: turning away from ordinary matters of the world in order to return to oneself, taking account of one's actions, reflecting on where one has been in the past year and where one is headed in the year to come. *Aséret Y'mey T'shuvah* — ten days of meeting oneself face-to-face, opening the heart to change.*

BETWEEN PAST AND FUTURE,
BETWEEN BIRTH AND DEATH

What does it mean to be "between," to dwell in the between?

In Hebrew, twilight is *beyn hash'mashot* — literally, "between the suns." So too in English: *twi-light*, two lights, or the "between-light," the light between night and day. Time that is neither day nor night but the span between them. Liminal time, the most evocative minutes of the twenty-four hours.

But is not all time liminal? Aren't we always poised just before what is about to happen? Positioned between dawn and dusk, dusk and dawn, we live between past and future because we cannot live *in* them; we cannot act in them or change their outcomes. In this sense, past and future don't exist for us; only the time between them — the present time — exists.

Yet the present is never captured or even grasped; no sooner is it here than it is gone. What, then, are we left with? What do we have?

If by "to have" we mean to possess, to keep, "to have and to hold," then truly we have nothing, because nothing in this life stays with us. How do we live with the knowledge not just of our own mortality but of the truth that we cannot hold on to anything? How do we keep from succumbing to despair?

*The concept of *t'shuvah* is discussed further in part 5, pages 214–218.

"All is vapor, nothing but vapors!" cries the author of Ecclesiastes. Nothing on earth is substantial. So, too, the eighteenth-century Japanese poet Issa laments, upon the death of his child, "The world of dew is a world of dew." Everything vanishes; there is no other reality.

Un'taneh Tókef K'dushat Hayom compares human life to "dry grass, withering blossoms, passing shadows, vanishing clouds, drifting wind, scattering dust, a fleeting dream."

The evanescence of time is a universal theme.

But Issa's poem does not stop there. It concludes, "And yet, and yet": nonetheless, we love. This is what it means to be human.

Un'taneh Tókef goes on to affirm that the source of all life exists in perpetuity and we are part of that greater wholeness: our names are linked to its name. Although we cannot hold on to any moment, we are alive in the ongoing flow of "between," from which we are inseparable. This too is what it means to be human. To be fully aware of our connectedness to everything in our world can bring serenity and fulfillment.

BETWEEN THE COVERS OF THIS BOOK

The Days Between is a companion for travelers on the to-and-fro journey of *Aséret Y'mey T'shuvah*, the Ten Days of Returning—inward to the self and outward to relationships between self and other. Like my previous book of liturgy, *The Book of Blessings*, this book re-creates Jewish prayer from an inclusive, nonhierarchical perspective. While all the offerings here, in Hebrew as well as English, are new, they are steeped in biblical and rabbinic themes and imagery.

There is no "God" in these pages—but every page, I

hope, evokes the sacred. *The Days Between* is for all those seeking to participate in Jewish civilization and culture without compromising intellectual or spiritual integrity. This includes nontheists as well as theists, those who identify as religious or spiritual, as well as those who call themselves secular or humanist. The High Holiday liturgy, with its emphasis on sin and judgment, can strike a discordant note even for those who pray regularly during the year. My intention in this book is to bring fresh language and meaning to the seasonal liturgy and to speak to the widest possible spectrum of Jews looking for a new experience of the High Holidays.

Three themes central to the traditional liturgy are at the core of this book: *t'shuvah*, *s'liḥah* (forgiveness), and mortality. *S'liḥah* here includes self-forgiveness, as well as the forgiveness we seek from others for our wrongs, missteps, and failings.

The book is in five parts, the first four of which are liturgy and the last an essay.

Parts 1 and 3, for Rosh Hashanah and Yom Kippur, respectively, offer bilingual (Hebrew and English) blessings and prayers for the home, the synagogue, and other individual and communal settings. The Hebrew and English are not exact equivalents but rather parallel passages; neither is a translation of the other. (In some cases, the English was written first; in other cases, the Hebrew.) Brief introductions precede several of the more complex liturgical offerings.

Part 1 opens with "Approaching the Gates," a set of blessings for the festive Rosh Hashanah meal. This is followed by "Opening the Heart," a selection of prayers based on core elements of the Rosh Hashanah synagogue service. Part 1 closes with "We Cast into the Depths of the Sea," a re-creation of the ritual of *Tashlikh*, which is customarily performed near a body of water on the first day of the holiday (on the second day, if the first day falls on the Sabbath).

Part 3 begins with "Gathering In," blessings for use in the home on Yom Kippur eve. "Turning the Heart," which focuses on key themes of the holy day, derives from segments of the synagogue services. It includes, among other offerings, a re-visioning of *Kol Nidrey*, the most famous—and perhaps most puzzling—moment of the High Holiday liturgy. The ritual commonly referred to as *Yizkor*, which honors deceased loved ones, is re-created with recitations, poems, and meditations in "Remembering the Lives." "*N'ilah*: Closing of the Gates" provides the denouement and ending of Yom Kippur. "From End to Beginning" is a transition back to secular time.

Part 2 of the book, "Window, Bird, Sky" (in English only), bridges Rosh Hashanah and Yom Kippur, touching on aspects of awareness not overtly given voice in parts 1 and 3. Comprising a Daily Psalm (poem) and a Direction of the Heart (prose meditation) for each of the Ten Days of Returning, this section is meant to support inner reflection and contemplation during the full span of the season, so that the holy days become the end points on a continuum of deepening *t'shuvah*.

Part 4 was composed in response to requests from various groups seeking innovative self-contained services. Toward this end, I arranged elements from parts 1, 2, and 3 into the service "Entering the Gates," for use on Rosh Hashanah and/or Yom Kippur.

Part 5, an essay on *Un'taneh Tókef K'dushat Hayom*, analyzes the complex structure and content of this key piece of liturgy and explores ways to reframe theological concepts found in it—concepts that echo throughout the High Holidays.

IT IS MY HOPE that *The Days Between*—whether used as alternative or supplement to the traditional liturgy, in synagogue pews or at the dinner table, by a riverbank or at a kitchen window—will bring light to the days and enrichment to the season. As the year turns yet again, may the heart, too, turn once more—to fresh beginnings and to the begetting of one's best self.

One ❦ Rosh Hashanah

ראש השנה

Approaching the Gates
Festive Meal for Rosh Hashanah Eve

לפני השער

סעודת ליל ראש השנה

הדלקת נרות לראש השנה

קוּמִי אוֹרִי כִּי בָא אוֹרֵךְ.
—ישעיה ס, א

יָאִיר לִבֵּנוּ,
תִּתְחַדֵּשׁ רוּחֵנוּ

בְּהַדְלָקַת נֵר שֶׁל יוֹם טוֹב
וּבְקַבָּלַת הַשָּׁנָה הַחֲדָשָׁה.

Lighting the Candles for Rosh Hashanah

Rise up, shine, for your light is here.
—Isaiah 60:1

May our hearts be lightened,
our spirits born anew

as we light the holiday candles
and greet the newborn year.

ברכת הזמן

הַמְשַׁלֵּחַ מַעְיָנִים בַּנְּחָלִים
בֵּין הָרִים יְהַלֵּכוּן.
—תהלים קד, י

נָבוֹא בִּשְׁעָרִים, מוֹדִים
עַל חֶסֶד הַהִתְחַדְּשׁוּת.

נְבָרֵךְ אֶת מַעְיַן חַיֵּינוּ
שֶׁהֶחֱיָנוּ וְקִיְּמָנוּ וְהִגִּיעָנוּ
לַזְּמַן הַזֶּה.

Blessing of Renewal

Springs and rivers gush forth,
flowing between the hills.
—Psalms 104:10

We enter the gates, grateful
for the blessing of renewal.

Let us bless the flow of life
that revives us,
sustains us,
and brings us to this time.

ברכת הבת, ברכת הבן

וּרְחֹבוֹת הָעִיר יִמָּלְאוּ
יְלָדִים וִילָדוֹת
מְשַׂחֲקִים בִּרְחֹבֹתֶיהָ.
‏—זכריה ח, ה

ברכת הבת

‏—[שם הילדה]

הֱיִי אֲשֶׁר תִּהְיִי
וַהֲיִי בְּרוּכָה
בַּאֲשֶׁר תִּהְיִי.

❧

ברכת הבן

‏—[שם הילד]

הֱיֵה אֲשֶׁר תִּהְיֶה
וֶהֱיֵה בָּרוּךְ
בַּאֲשֶׁר תִּהְיֶה.

Blessing the Children

The squares of the city will be filled
with boys and girls playing.
— Zechariah 8:5

[The child's name] —

Be who you are,
and may you be blessed
in all that you are.

ברכת פרי הגפן

וְיַיִן יְשַׂמַּח לְבַב־אֱנוֹשׁ.
—תהלים קד, טו

בְּיוֹם הַזִּכָּרוֹן
נִזְכֹּר דּוֹרוֹת עוֹלָם,

בְּיוֹם תְּרוּעָה
נִשְׁמַע קוֹל דְּמָמָה,

בְּיוֹם הֲרַת עוֹלָם
נַתְחִיל מִבְּרֵאשִׁית.

נְבָרֵךְ אֶת עֵין הַחַיִּים
הַמְפַכָּה לְלֹא הֲפוּגָה
וּמַצְמִיחָה אֶת פְּרִי הַגָּפֶן.

Fruit of the Vine

Wine makes the heart joyful.
— Psalms 104:15

On this Day of Remembering
we recall the generations.

On this Day of the Shofar's sounding
we listen for the voices within.

On this Birthday of the World
we start anew.

Let us hallow this day, as we bless
the ever-flowing wellspring
that nourishes fruit on the vine.

ברכת פרי העץ: תפוח בדבש

וְעֵץ הַשָּׂדֶה יִתֵּן פְּרְיוֹ.
—ויקרא כו, ד

לְכוּ אִכְלוּ מַשְׁמַנִּים
וּשְׁתוּ מַמְתַקִּים
וְשִׁלְחוּ מָנוֹת לְאֵין נָכוֹן לוֹ
כִּי־קָדוֹשׁ הַיּוֹם.
—נחמיה ח, י

נְבָרֵךְ אֶת עֵין הַחַיִּים
הַמְמַלְּאָה אֶת פְּרִי הָעֵץ
בְּמֶתֶק.

תְּהֵא הַשָּׁנָה מְתוּקָה
כְּתַפּוּחַ בִּדְבַשׁ
וּמְלֵאָה בְּרָכוֹת כְּרִמּוֹן.

Fruit of the Tree: Apples and Honey

The trees of the field
will give forth their fruit.
— Leviticus 26:4

Go, eat choice foods
and drink sweet drinks
and send portions to those
who have not provided for themselves,
for the day is holy.
— Nehemiah 8:10

Let us bless the source of life
that swells the tree's fruit with sweetness.

May the year be sweet as apples dipped in honey
and full as the ripe pomegranate
with blessings.

It is customary to eat various specific foods at the Rosh Hashanah evening meal. Apples dipped in honey symbolize a sweet new year; the many-seeded pomegranate is a symbol of abundance. Certain vegetables that grow directly from the ground, such as pumpkins, beets, and leeks — "fruits of the earth" — are also customarily eaten. "Fruit of the Tree: Apples and Honey" and the blessing that follows it, "Fruits of the Earth," are provided for these customs, which have their origin in the Talmud (b. Keritot 6a).

ברכת פרי האדמה

וְנָתְנָה הָאָרֶץ יְבוּלָהּ.
—ויקרא כו, ד

נְבָרֵךְ אֶת עֵין הַחַיִּים
הַמַּרְבָּה אֶת פְּרִי הָאֲדָמָה.

Fruits of the Earth

The land will yield its bounty.
— Leviticus 26:4

Let us bless the wellspring
that nurtures to fullness
the fruits of the earth.

נטילת ידיים

אֶרְחַץ בְּנִקָּיוֹן כַּפָּי.

—תהלים כו, ו

תִּזְכֹּר נַפְשֵׁנוּ
אֶת קְדֻשַּׁת הַגּוּף
בִּנְטִילַת יָדַיִם.

Washing the Hands

I will wash my palms
in innocence.
— Psalms 26:6

Washing the hands,
we call to mind
the holiness of body.

ברכת הלחם

וְלֶחֶם לְבַב־אֱנוֹשׁ יִסְעָד.
—תהלים קד, טו

נְבָרֵךְ אֶת עֵין הַחַיִּים
הַמּוֹצִיאָה לֶחֶם מִן הָאָרֶץ.

Blessing before the Meal

Bread is the sustenance of the heart.
— Psalms 104:15

Let us bless the source of life
that brings forth bread from the earth.

ברכת המזון

וַאֲכַלְתֶּם לַחְמְכֶם לָשֹׂבַע
וִישַׁבְתֶּם לָבֶטַח בְּאַרְצְכֶם.
—ויקרא כו, ה

כִּי־יִהְיֶה בְךָ אֶבְיוֹן . . .
פָּתֹחַ תִּפְתַּח אֶת־יָדְךָ לוֹ.
—דברים טו, ז–ח

נוֹדֶה לְעֵין הַחַיִּים
הַזָּנָה אֶת הַכֹּל.

נִשְׁמֹר עַל הָאָרֶץ
הַטּוֹבָה וְהָרְחָבָה
וְהִיא תְּקַיְּמֵנוּ

וּנְבַקֵּשׁ שִׂבְעַת לֶחֶם
לְכָל הַדָּרִים בָּהּ.

Blessing after the Meal

You will eat your fill of bread
and dwell securely on the land.
—Leviticus 26:5

If there is a needy person among you . . .
open your hand and give.
—Deuteronomy 15:7–8

We are grateful for the riches
of the good, giving earth.

We will tend the earth's gifts,
that they may flourish,

and seek sustenance for all
who dwell here with us.

Opening the Heart

❦

פתיחת הלב

פְּתִיחַת הַלֵּב

לִתְשׁוּבַת הַשָּׁנָה
בַּיָּמִים שֶׁבֵּין לְבֵין
נִפְנֶה עֹרֶף לַיָּדוּעַ

חַלּוֹן וְחָצֵר
גַּג וְגָדֵר

וְנִפְסַע בִּשְׁבִילִים
שֶׁטֶּרֶם נִתַּן
לְקָרְאָם בְּשֵׁם.

עָנָן וְשָׁמַיִם
עֲרִיפִים וּכְנָפַיִם

אַט אַט
יִפָּרְמוּ הַתְּפָרִים,
הַקָּשֶׁה יֵרֵךְ

סוּף וְשִׂיחַ
נַחַל וְרוּחַ

וְלֵב סָגוּר יִפָּתַח
לִסְלִיחָה.

Opening the Heart

At the year's turn
in the days between

we step away
from what we know

> *wall and window*
> *roof and road*

into the spaces
we cannot yet name

> *cloud and sky*
> *cloud and wings*

Slowly the edges
begin to yield

the hard places
soften

> *wind and clover*
> *reed and river*

The gate to forgiveness
opens

Introduction to *Un'taneh Tókef K'dushat Hayom*: We Declare the Utter Sanctity of This Day

"*Un'taneh Tókef K'dushat Hayom*: We Declare the Utter Sanctity of This Day" — a core passage of the Rosh Hashanah and Yom Kippur services in the Ashkenazic rite — has captured the Jewish imagination for centuries, despite being difficult to penetrate, structurally complex, and theologically challenging.* Lengthy and multi-sectioned, it reads more like a poetic collage than a unified composition. The frame of the collage is the theme of judgment: God is extolled as Judge and Ruler; we pass before His scrutinizing gaze like sheep; our destiny lies in His hands.† For many readers today, the theology of reward and punishment is not a helpful guide for living one's life. Yet *Un'taneh Tókef* (it is most often referred to by its initial two words) compels and, some might say, haunts us: it has a mysterious, almost eerie, quality that makes it difficult to set aside. And so, century after century, we continue to turn back to it — in the words of the rabbis, to "turn it and turn it."‡

One "turning" — one more way to draw meaning from this ancient text — would be to set aside its frame and focus on the picture inside: the image of death. Who will live and who will die, who now and who later, when and by what

---

*A fuller discussion of *Un'taneh Tókef* may be found in part 5, which begins on page 205.

†Here and throughout, references to God as personified or gendered reflect the language and theology of the texts being quoted or paraphrased, not the perspective of this book.

‡The talmudic dictum "Turn it and turn it" (Pirkey Avot 5:22) refers to the study of Torah, which the rabbis encourage one to do over and over again, in order to fully grasp its meaning.

means will each of us come to our end? For the one certainty in life is that we *will* come to our end: all is ephemeral, all is fading, nothing that lives is unchanging. All religions grapple with the ultimate fact of our mortality and the mortality of everyone and everything we love. In Jewish liturgy, no other passage is as forthright as *Un'taneh Tókef* in laying this truth before us. Its unique combination of poignancy and bluntness accounts in good measure, I believe, for its power.

And it is this power that makes *Un'taneh Tókef* so fitting to the turning of the year, the period in which we confront death and dying most pointedly. With the changing of the seasons and (in the Northern Hemisphere) the waning of daylight, we become especially aware of the passage of time in the natural world. So too, as we start a new year, with its promise of renewal and fresh beginnings, we become more alert to the workings of time in our personal lives.

Un'taneh Tókef brings death and loss into the forefront of our awareness, giving voice to our fears while placing our deaths in the larger context of all that lives. The re-creation offered here highlights those aspects of *Un'taneh Tókef* that I believe are most useful for confronting our mortality.

ונתנה תוקף קדושת היום

וּנְתַנֶּה תֹקֶף קְדֻשַּׁת הַיּוֹם
כִּי הוּא נוֹרָא וְאָיֹם.

וּבְשׁוֹפָר גָּדוֹל יִתָּקַע
וְקוֹל דְּמָמָה דַּקָּה יִשָּׁמַע.

קוֹל אֱנוֹשׁ—
קָנֶה בְּיַם הַסּוּף,
נְשִׁיפָה בָּרוּחַ.

בְּרֹאשׁ הַשָּׁנָה יִכָּתֵבוּן
וּבְיוֹם צוֹם כִּפּוּר יֵחָתֵמוּן.

חַיֵּינוּ סְפוּרִים
חֲקוּקִים בַּזְּמַן.

בִּתְשׁוּבַת הַשָּׁנָה
נַבִּיט קֶדֶם וְאָחוֹר,

נִזְכֹּר כִּי כָּל יָמֵינוּ
יָמִים שֶׁבֵּין לְבֵין.

Un'taneh Tókef K'dushat Hayom:
We Declare the Utter Sanctity of This Day

Un'taneh tókef k'dushat hayom
ki hu nora v'ayom.

Uv'shofar gadol yitaka
v'kol d'mamah dakah yishama.

We declare the utter sanctity of this day
for it is an awe-filled day.

A great shofar is sounded
and a voice of slender silence is heard.

> The voice is one's own —
> a reed in the chorus,
> a breath in the wind.

❧

B'rosh hashanah yikateyvun
uv'yom tzom kipur yeyḥateymun.

On Rosh Hashanah it is written
and on Yom Kippur it is sealed.

> Our lives are stories
> inscribed in time.
>
> At the turning of the year
> we look back, look ahead, see
>
> that we are always
> in the days between:

כַּמָּה יַעַבְרוּן וְכַמָּה יִבָּרֵאוּן,
מִי יִחְיֶה וּמִי יָמוּת,
מִי בְקִצּוֹ וּמִי לֹא בְקִצּוֹ,
מִי בַמַּיִם וּמִי בָאֵשׁ,
מִי בַחֶרֶב וּמִי בַחַיָּה,
מִי בָרָעָב וּמִי בַצָּמָא,
מִי בָרַעַשׁ וּמִי בַמַּגֵּפָה,
מִי בַחֲנִיקָה וּמִי בַסְּקִילָה,
מִי יָנוּחַ וּמִי יָנוּעַ,
מִי יִשָּׁקֵט וּמִי יִטָּרֵף
מִי יִשָּׁלֵו וּמִי יִתְיַסָּר,
מִי יָרוּם וּמִי יִשָּׁפֵל,
מִי יַעֲשִׁיר וּמִי יַעֲנִי.

❧

וּתְשׁוּבָה
וּתְפִלָּה
וּצְדָקָה
מַעֲבִירִין אֶת־רֹעַ הַגְּזֵרָה.

How many will leave this life
and how many will be born into it,
who will live and who will die,
whose life will reach its natural end
and whose will be cut short,
who by water and who by fire,
who by sword and who by beast,
who by hunger and who by thirst,
who by quake and who by plague,
who by choking and who by stoning,
who will rest and who will wander,
who will be tranquil and who will be torn,
who will be at peace and who will be tormented,
who will be raised high and who will be brought low,
who will prosper and who will be impoverished.

Ut'shuvah
Turning inward
to face one's self

Ut'filah
Entering into prayer
and contemplation

Utz'dakah
Giving to the needy,
as justice requires

Ma'avirin et-ró'a hag'zerah
These diminish the harshness
of the decree

וּתְשׁוּבָה

לָשׁוּב אֶל לִבַּת הַיְצִירָה
הַצָּרָה צוּרָה
לְכָל חַי וָחַי,

וּתְפִלָּה

לְהִתְעוֹרֵר אֶל זְרִימָה
שֶׁאֵינָהּ פּוֹסֶקֶת
בְּתוֹכֵנוּ וּסְבִיבֵנוּ,

לַחֲבֹק אֶת הַיֹּפִי הַחוֹלֵף,

וּצְדָקָה

לָדַעַת כִּי אָנוּ כֻּלָּנוּ
בָּשָׂר וָדָם
וְחַיֵּינוּ אֲרוּגִים—
מָתוֹק וּמַר,
מַר וּמָלוּחַ—

וּפְרִי הַחֶסֶד
חֶסֶד,
וּמַעֲשִׂים טוֹבִים
פָּעֳלוֹ,

מַעֲבִירִין אֶת־רֹעַ הַגְּזֵרָה.

נִתְבָּרֵךְ בְּעֹשֶׁר חַיֵּינוּ,
נִגְבֹּר עַל אֵימַת הֶעָתִיד.

Ut'shuvah
> Returning to the inner artistry
> that gives each life its form,
>
> seeking to become
> one's truest self

Ut'filah
> Being alive to the unending flow
> within and around us,
>
> holding dear
> the transient beauty

Utz'dakah
> Knowing that we are, all of us,
> flesh and blood
>
> and our fates are intertwined —
> sweet with bitter, bitter with salt —
>
> and that the fruit of kindness
> is kindness,
>
> and good deeds
> are its fulfillment

Ma'avirin et-ró'a hag'zerah
> We become present
> to the fullness of our lives
>
> and untether ourselves from the fear
> of what lies ahead

❧

יְסוֹדֵנוּ מֵעָפָר וְסוֹפֵנוּ לֶעָפָר.
בְּנַפְשֵׁנוּ נָבִיא לַחְמֵנוּ.

אָנוּ מְשׁוּלִים כַּחֶרֶס הַנִּשְׁבָּר,
כֶּחָצִיר יָבֵשׁ וּכְצִיץ נוֹבֵל,
כְּצֵל עוֹבֵר וּכְעָנָן כָּלֶה
וּכְרוּחַ נוֹשֶׁבֶת וּכְאָבָק פּוֹרֵחַ
וְכַחֲלוֹם יָעוּף.

נוֹלַדְנוּ לַבְּרִיאָה
הַנּוֹשֵׂאת אוֹתָנוּ בְּחֵיקָה
וּבְחִבּוּקָהּ נָמוּת.

הַשָּׁלֵם יִכּוֹן לָעַד.
אֵין קֵץ לַנִּסְתָּר בּוֹ,
אֵין שִׁעוּר לְגְלוּיָּיו,
אֵין קִצְבָּה לִשְׁנוֹתָיו.

גַּם בְּמוֹתֵנוּ
יִזָּכְרוּ כָּל שְׁמוֹתֵינוּ
בַּשָּׁלֵם הַגָּדוֹל.

וּנְתַנֶּה תֹקֶף קְדֻשַּׁת הַיּוֹם.

We begin in earth
and we end in earth.
We spend our lives earning our bread.
We are like broken vessels,
dry grass, withering blossoms,
passing shadows, vanishing clouds,
drifting wind, scattering dust,
a fleeting dream.

> Born in nature
> and borne by nature,
> we die in its lap-and-fold.

> The whole lives on,
> infinite in mystery,
> its manifestations numberless.

> Seeing beyond our separate deaths,
> we find our selves in the greater whole,
> our names embedded in its names,
> its names embedded in ours.

Un'taneh tókef k'dushat hayom.

We proclaim the powerful sanctity
of this day.

The flush-left English lines in this poem are transliterations, new translations, or adaptations of key lines in the traditional Hebrew text. The
indented lines are wholly new additions, amplifying the meanings of
the traditional prayer. *Un'taneh Tókef* is recited on Rosh Hashanah and
again on Yom Kippur.

Introduction to *Shofarot, Zikhronot, Malkhuyot*: Calls, Recalling, Callings

Unique to the Rosh Hashanah service are three extended liturgical passages—*Malkhuyot, Zikhronot,* and *Shofarot*—each comprising a rabbinic poetic prologue, ten biblical verses, and a concluding petition and blessing. After the reading of each passage, the shofar is sounded.

The themes of the traditional passages, in their original order, are as follows:

Malkhuyot (literally, "sovereignty"): God as ruler and creator; God's power over all creation and, by extension, His role as judge of our actions.* The tenth biblical verse of *Malkhuyot* is Judaism's keynote, commonly referred to as the *Sh'ma*: *Sh'ma, yisra'eyl, adonay elohéynu, adonay eḥad,* "Hear, O Israel, the Lord is our God, the Lord is one" (Deuteronomy 6:4), emphasizing God's singular dominion over all.

Zikhronot (literally, "remembrances"): God's remembering (taking account of, being attentive to) all creatures, and His fidelity to His covenant with the people of Israel.

Shofarot (literally, "rams' horns"): The shofar calls out, and we hark to it. Some of the biblical verses describe with dramatic force God's revelation of Himself to the world and His giving of the Ten Commandments to Israel. Other verses proclaim the

---

*References to God as personified or gendered reflect the language and theology of the texts being quoted or paraphrased, not the perspective of this book.

advent of the festivals, including the New Moon and Rosh Hashanah.

The re-creation offered here reorders the sequence to create a progression of awareness. Each section is interpreted afresh, emphasizing the twin focus of the holiday: looking inward, to better know oneself, and looking outward, to strengthen one's relations with others. I have distilled the liturgical text to a few of its key biblical verses (the *Sh'ma* is adapted), augmenting them with brief reflections. To these elements I have added Deuteronomy 30:12–14 and a poem.

The themes are re-visioned as follows:

Shofarot (Calls): The call to awakening the self and to hearing others.

Zikhronot (Recalling): Memory, imagination, and the forming of the self; the emergence of relationships.

Malkhuyot (Callings): The values we hold above all else. The *Sh'ma* is reframed: finding our place in the greater one-ness.

שׁוֹפְרוֹת

תִּקְעוּ בַחֹדֶשׁ שׁוֹפָר,
בַּכֶּסֶה לְיוֹם חַגֵּנוּ.
—תהלים פא, ד

קוֹל הַשּׁוֹפָר נִשְׁמָע:
הַשָּׁנָה הַחֲדָשָׁה בַּפֶּתַח.

❧

כָּל־יֹשְׁבֵי תֵבֵל וְשֹׁכְנֵי אָרֶץ.
כִּנְשֹׂא־נֵס הָרִים תִּרְאוּ
וְכִתְקֹעַ שׁוֹפָר תִּשְׁמָעוּ.
—ישעיה יח, ג

קוֹל הַשּׁוֹפָר קוֹרֵא,
מַשְׁקִיט אֶת רוּחֵנוּ,
מֵעִיר בָּנוּ קוֹל דְּמָמָה.

❧

בְּקָרַחַת הַיַּעַר
שָׁם הַנֶּפֶשׁ פּוֹרַחַת
וְהָעוֹלָם כֻּלוֹ מֵנֵץ,
שִׁמְעוּ
לַקּוֹל בַּשִּׂיחִים
מֵעֵבֶר לַדֶּשֶׁא.

הַאֲזִינוּ:
הָאִלֵּם מַבִּיעַ אֹמֶר.

Shofarot: Calls
HEARING AND ATTENDING

Sound the shofar on the New Moon,
on our holiday, when the moon is still hidden.
— Psalms 81:4

> The shofar calls, the crescent rises.
> The new year is upon us.

🕭

O inhabitants of the world,
you who dwell upon the earth:
When the flag is raised on the mountain — look!
When the shofar is sounded — listen!
— Isaiah 18:3

> The shofar quiets us, wakening us
> to the silence within.

🕭

In the clearing, where the mind flowers
and the world sprouts up at every side,
listen
for the sound in the bushes,
behind the grass.

> The shofar takes us into the self
> that is hidden from the self,
> then returns us to the world.
> In the silence we hear the voice of the other,
> we hear what has gone unheard.

הַזִּכָּרוֹן מְגַלֶּה לָנוּ
מִי אָנוּ.
הַדִּמְיוֹן לָשׁ אוֹתוֹ
בְּכָל רֶגַע מֵחָדָשׁ.
בְּכָל רֶגַע, הָאֲנִי
לוֹבֵשׁ פָּנִים חֲדָשׁוֹת.

❦

זָכַרְתִּי לָךְ חֶסֶד נְעוּרַיִךְ,
אַהֲבַת כְּלוּלֹתָיִךְ,
לֶכְתֵּךְ אַחֲרַי בַּמִּדְבָּר,
בְּאֶרֶץ לֹא זְרוּעָה.
—ירמיה ב, ב

מִיַּלְדוּת וְעַד זִקְנָה,
הַקֶּשֶׁר עִם הַזּוּלָת
הוֹלֵךְ וּמַעֲמִיק.

❦

וְזָכַרְתִּי אֲנִי אֶת־בְּרִיתִי אוֹתָךְ
בִּימֵי נְעוּרָיִךְ
וַהֲקִימוֹתִי לָךְ בְּרִית עוֹלָם.
—יחזקאל טז, ס

מִי יִתֵּן וְכָל קְשָׁרֵינוּ
יִהְיוּ כֵּנִים,
הֲדָדִיִּים,
נֶאֱמָנִים.

Zikhronot: Recalling

MEMORY, SELF, AND OTHER

> Recollections shape us, remind us who we are.
> Imagination brings what is buried
> to light.
>
> With each moment recalled,
> the kaleidoscope turns,
> patterns change, colors shift places.
> The selves within the self come into view.

❧

I remember the lovingkindness of your youthful days,
your love when you were betrothed,
when you followed me in the wilderness,
in the land barren of seed.
—Jeremiah 2:2

> From youth to age,
> our bonds with others deepen,
> become more truthful.

❧

I will remember my covenant with you
from the days of your youth
and I will establish that covenant for eternity.
—Ezekiel 16:60

> Reciprocity, fidelity:
> the grounding of relationship.

מלכויות

שְׂאוּ שְׁעָרִים רָאשֵׁיכֶם
וְהִנָּשְׂאוּ פִּתְחֵי עוֹלָם.
—תהלים כד, ז

הַשְׁעָרִים פְּתוּחִים
לְשִׁפְעַת אֶפְשָׁרִיּוֹת:
נִשָּׂא עֵינֵינוּ אֲלֵיהֶן.

❧

לֹא בַשָּׁמַיִם הוּא לֵאמֹר:
מִי יַעֲלֶה־לָּנוּ הַשָּׁמַיְמָה וְיִקָּחֶהָ לָּנוּ, וְיַשְׁמִעֵנוּ אֹתָהּ,
וְנַעֲשֶׂנָּה?

וְלֹא־מֵעֵבֶר לַיָּם הוּא לֵאמֹר:
מִי יַעֲבָר־לָנוּ אֶל־עֵבֶר הַיָּם וְיִקָּחֶהָ לָּנוּ, וְיַשְׁמִעֵנוּ אֹתָהּ,
וְנַעֲשֶׂנָּה?

כִּי־קָרוֹב אֵלֶיךָ הַדָּבָר מְאֹד,
בְּפִיךָ וּבִלְבָבְךָ, לַעֲשֹׂתוֹ.
—דברים ל, יב-יד

נִתְבּוֹנֵן פְּנִימָה.
נְצַפֶּה לְגִלּוּי יְעוּדֵנוּ.

❧

שְׁמַע, יִשְׂרָאֵל:
הַקְּדֻשָּׁה שׁוֹפַעַת בַּכֹּל,

Malkhuyot: Callings

SELF AND ONE

Lift up high, O gates,
lift the eternal portals!
— Psalms 24:7

> The gates are open, portals
> to possibilities:
> What is it that reigns for us supreme?

❧

It is not in the heavens, such that you might say:
Who among us can go up and get it for us and let us hear it
so that we may do it?

And it is not across the sea, such that you might say:
Who will cross the sea for us and get it for us and let us hear it
so that we may do it?

No, it is something very close to you,
in your mouth and in your heart,
for you to do.
— Deuteronomy 30:12–14

> We turn back to ourselves,
> listen for our callings.

❧

Hear, O Israel —

The divine abounds everywhere
and dwells in everything.

אַלְפֵי רְבָבָה פָּנֶיהָ,
מְלֹא עוֹלָם שְׁכִינָתָה.

הַכֹּל אֶחָד.
—בעקבות דברים ו, ד

Its faces are infinite,
its source suffuses all.

The many are One.
—Adapted from Deuteronomy 6:4

תהא

תְּהֵא הַשָּׁנָה הַזֹּאת
טוֹבָה וּמְלֵאָה בְּרָכוֹת:

בִּרְכַּת **אַהֲבָה**,
בְּרִיאוּת וּגְדִילָה,
דַּעַת וְהַשְׁרָאָה,
וִתּוּר, זֹךְ וָחֶסֶד,
טַעַם וִידִידוּת,

בִּרְכַּת **כָּ**בוֹד,
לִמּוּד, **מַזָּל**,
נַחַת וְסוֹבְלָנוּת,
עֹנֶג, **פַּ**רְנָסָה, **צְ**דָקָה,
קֹרַת רוּחַ וְ**קִ**רְבָה,

בִּרְכַּת **רַ**חֲמִים וּרְפוּאָה,
שָׁלוֹם וְ**שַׁ**לְוָה,
שָׂשׂוֹן וְ**שִׂ**מְחָה,
תִּקְוָה וּתְהִלָּה.

לוּ נִזְכֶּה לְשָׁנָה טוֹבָה.

May It Be So

May the year bring abundant blessings —
beauty, creativity, delight!

May we be confident, courageous,
and devoted to our callings.

May our lives be enriched with education.
May we find enjoyment in our work
and fulfillment in our friendships.

May we grow, may we have good health.
In darker times, may we be sustained
by gratitude and hope.

May we be infused with joy.
May we know intimacy and kindness,
may we love without limit.

May the hours be enhanced with music
and nurtured by art.
May our endeavors be marked by originality.

May we take pleasure in daily living.
May we find peace within ourselves
and help peace emerge in the world.

May we receive the gifts of quiet.

May reason guide our choices,
may romance grace our lives.

May our spirits be serene,
may we find solace in solitude.

May we embrace tolerance and truth
and the understanding that underlies both.

May we be inspired with **v**ision and **w**onder,
may we be open to e**x**ploration.

May our deepest **y**earnings be fulfilled,
may we be suffused with **z**eal for life.

May we merit these blessings
and may they come to be.
May it be so.

"May It Be So" and its Hebrew counterpart are abecedarian poems,
a type of acrostic in which the initial letters of key words appear in
alphabetical succession. Abecedarians were a popular form of *piyyut*
(liturgical poetry) composed for Rosh Hashanah and Yom Kippur,
typically to delineate sins or to enumerate God's attributes. These new
English and Hebrew abecedarians express wishes, hopes, and blessings.

We Cast into the Depths of the Sea

(*Tashlikh* Ritual)

נשליך במצולות ים

Introduction

The ritual commonly known as *Tashlikh*—literally, "You [God] will cast"—takes its name from Micah 7:19: *V'tashlikh bim'tzulot yam kol-ḥatotam*, "You will cast [hurl, cast away] all their sins into the depths of the sea." Performed on the afternoon of the first day of Rosh Hashanah (or on the second day, if the first day falls on the Sabbath), *Tashlikh* takes place near an ocean, river, or other natural body of water. After the recitation of the verse from Micah, crusts or crumbs of bread are tossed into the water to symbolically cast one's sins away.

The re-created ritual, "We Cast into the Depths of the Sea," begins with "Casting Away," a recitation that revisions and expands upon the theme of the biblical verse. The opening word in the Hebrew is *nashlikh*, "we will cast [away]." Instead of asking that God purge us of sin, we seek in this declaration to free ourselves from whatever impedes our moving into the new year with clarity, lightness, and hope.

"Poems of the River and the Sea" accompanies "Casting Away." This section includes Hebrew poems by Zelda (Mishkovsky) and Leah Goldberg, and a Yiddish poem by Malka Heifetz Tussman, along with my English translations. In each poem, water is an image at once revelatory, transformative, and redemptive. There are other common threads among the poems: each explores time, change, and mortality in the context of intimate relationships; and in each, water is given a voice. Zelda's sea sings, Goldberg's river hums, Tussman's creek babbles.

The speaker of Zelda's "Facing the Sea" gives herself over to the sea's consoling embrace. Although the sea laughs and she sorrows, they sing in unison of the soul's immortality.

So, too, self and other are united in Leah Goldberg's "The Blade of Grass Sings to the River" and "The Tree Sings to the River." Reflected in the great body of the river, the blade is "swallowed up" and "erased": the small self dissolves into the larger wholeness. In the latter poem, river and tree stream together as siblings, the one providing song and time to the other's budding and fruiting.

Like Goldberg's blade of grass, the speaker of Malka Heifetz Tussman's "Today Is Forever" looks into the water and sees herself reflected there. When she asks the creek whether it will flow in perpetuity — a way of asking about her own mortality — it answers her, laughing, as joyful as Zelda's laughing sea. The speaker responds with a smile.

נשליך

נַשְׁלִיךְ בִּמְצוּלוֹת יָם
חֵטְא, שְׁגָגָה וַחֲרָטָה.

בְּבוּאוֹת חֶסְרוֹן וּמְעִידָה
יָמוֹגוּ, יֵעָלְמוּ.

מָה נוּכַל לָשֵׂאת,
מָה נוּכַל לְהַשִּׁיל?

נִצָּלֵל בָּאֲפֵלָה,
נַהֲפֹךְ חֹשֶׁךְ לְאוֹר.

אֵילוּ מַכְאוֹבִים
עֲדַיִן אֲצוּרִים בָּנוּ?

אֵילוּ פְּצָעִים
טֶרֶם נִרְפְּאוּ?

נִפְתַּח אֶת יָדֵינוּ, נַפִּיל
אֶת שְׂרִידֵי הַבּוּשָׁה

וְנַתִּיר יֵאוּשׁ וָפַחַד
אֲשֶׁר נְטוּעִים בְּקִרְבֵּנוּ.

יָדַיִם פְּתוּחוֹת,
לֵב נִפְתָּח.

שָׁנָה חוֹלֶפֶת,
שָׁנָה קְרֵבָה.

Casting Away

We cast into the depths of the sea
our sins, and failures, and regrets.

Reflections of our imperfect selves
flow away.

> What can we bear,
> with what can we bear to part?

We upturn the darkness,
bring what is buried to light.

> What hurts still lodge,
> what wounds have yet to heal?

We empty our hands,
release the remnants of shame,

let go fear and despair
that have dug their home in us.

> Open hands,
> opening heart —

The year flows out,
the year flows in.

מול הים

כַּאֲשֶׁר שִׁחְרַרְתִּי אֶת דַּג הַזָּהָב
צָחַק הַיָּם
וְאִמֵּץ אוֹתִי
אֶל לִבּוֹ הַחָפְשִׁי,
אֶל לִבּוֹ הַזּוֹרֵם.
אָז שַׁרְנוּ יַחַד
(אֲנִי וְהוּא):
לֹא תָמוּת נַפְשִׁי. הֲיִשְׁלַט רָקָב
בְּזֶרֶם חַי?
הוּא שָׁר כָּךְ
עַל נַפְשׁוֹ הַסּוֹאֶנֶת,
וְאָנֹכִי שַׁרְתִּי
עַל נַפְשִׁי הַכּוֹאֶבֶת.

—זלדה

Facing the Sea

When I set free
the golden fish,

the sea laughed
and held me close

to his open heart,
to his streaming heart.

Then we sang together,
he and I:

My soul will not die.
Can decay rule a living stream?

So he sang
of his clamoring soul

and I sang
of my soul in pain.

—Zelda (trans. MF)

גבעול הדשא שר לנחל

גַּם לַקְּטַנִּים כָּמוֹנִי,
אֶחָד מִנִּי רְבָבָה
גַּם לְיַלְדֵי הָעֹנִי
עַל חוֹף הָאַכְזָבָה
הוֹמֶה, הוֹמֶה הַנַּחַל,
הוֹמֶה בְּאַהֲבָה.

הַשֶּׁמֶשׁ הַלּוֹטֶפֶת
תִּגַּע בּוֹ לִפְרָקִים,
וְגַם דְּמוּתִי נִשְׁקֶפֶת
בְּמַיִם יְרַקִּים,
וּבִמְצוּלַת הַנַּחַל
כֻּלָּנוּ עֲמֻקִּים.

דְּמוּתִי הַמִּתְעַמֶּקֶת
בַּדֶּרֶךְ אֶל הַיָּם
נִבְלַעַת וְנִמְחֶקֶת
עַל סַף הַנֶּעֱלָם.
וְעִם קוֹלוֹ שֶׁל נַחַל
הַנֶּפֶשׁ הַשּׁוֹתֶקֶת
עִם שִׁיר מִזְמוֹר הַנַּחַל
תַּגִּיד שִׁבְחֵי עוֹלָם.

—לאה גולדברג

The Blade of Grass Sings to the River

Even for the little ones like me,
one among the throng,
for the children of poverty
on disappointment's shore,
the river hums its song,
lovingly hums its song.

The sun's soft caress
touches it now and then.
My image, too, is reflected
in waters that flow green,
and in the river's depths
each one of us is deep.

My ever-deepening image
streaming away to the sea
is swallowed up, erased
on the edge of vanishing.
And with the river's voice,
with the river's psalm,
the speechless soul will sing
praises of the world.

— Leah Goldberg (trans. MF)

הָעֵץ שָׁר לַנַחַל

אֲשֶׁר נָשָׂא אֶת סְתָוֵי הַזָּהוֹב,
אֶת דָּמִי בַּשַּׁלֶּכֶת גָּרַף,
אֲשֶׁר יִרְאֶה אֲבִיבִי כִּי יָשׁוּב
עִם תְּקוּפַת הַשָּׁנָה אֵלָיו,

אֲחִי הַנַּחַל, הָאוֹבֵד לָעַד,
הֶחָדָשׁ יוֹם־יוֹם וְאַחֵר וְאֶחָד,
אֲחִי הַזֶּרֶם בֵּין שְׁנֵי חוֹפָיו
הַזּוֹרֵם כָּמוֹנִי בֵּין אָבִיב וּסְתָו.

כִּי אֲנִי הַנִּצָּן וַאֲנִי הַפְּרִי,
אֲנִי עֲתִידִי וַאֲנִי עֲבָרִי,
אֲנִי הַגֶּזַע הָעֲרִירִי,
וְאַתָּה—זְמַנִּי וְשִׁירִי.

—לאה גולדברג

The Tree Sings to the River

He who carried off my golden autumn,
who with the leaf-fall swept my blood away,
he who will see my spring return
to him, at the turning of the year —

my brother the river, forever lost,
new each day, and changed, and the same,
my brother the stream, between his two banks
streaming like me, between autumn and spring.

For I am the bud and I am the fruit,
I am my future and I am my past,
I am the solitary tree trunk,
and you — my time and my song.

— Leah Goldberg (trans. MF)

פֿון הײַנט איז אײביק

אָפֿט איך שפּאַציר אין נאָענטן פּאַרקל:
אַלטע ביימער מגושמדיק צעוואָקסן,
קוסטן, בלומען אין צעבלי פֿאַר אַלע פֿיר סעזאָנען,
אַ וואַסערל וואָס בולבלט קינדיש איבער שטיינדלעך,
אַ בריקל מיט ניט-געהובלטע פּאַרענטשן—
דאָס איז מײַן קליינער פּאַרקל.

מילד איז מיר און לינד איז מיר
אין אָטעם-ניגון פֿונעם פּאַרק
און גוט איז אויפֿכאַפּן אַ ביסעלע רכילות
פֿון פֿלי-און-פֿלאַטערוואַרג.

אָנגעלענט אָן פּלויטל,
זיך שפּיגלענדיק אין וואַסער לויטער,
איך פֿרעג:
וועסטו, ריטשקעלע, דאָ בײַכלען, טײַכלען
אייביק?
בולבלט לאַכנדיק דאָס טײַכל:
,,הײַנט איז אײביק.
אייביק איז אָט איצט".

שמייכל איך אַ פֿונקל גלייביק
און אַ זיפֿצעלע ניט גלייביק:
הײַנט איז אײביק.
אייביק איז אָט איצט.

—מלכּה חפֿץ טוזמאַן

From Today Is Forever

I stroll often in a nearby park —
old trees wildly overgrown,
bushes and flowers blooming all four seasons,
a creek babbling childishly over pebbles,
a small bridge with rough-hewn railings —
this is my little park.

It's mild and gentle
in the breath-song of the park
and good to catch some gossip
from the flutterers and fliers.

Leaning on the railing of the bridge,
seeing myself in clear water,
I ask, *Little stream,*
will you tumble and flow here
forever?

The creek babbles back, laughing,
Today is forever.
Forever is right now.

I smile, a sparkful of believing,
a sighful of not-believing:
Today is forever.
Forever is right now . . .

— Malka Heifetz Tussman (trans. MF)

Two ❦ Window, Bird, Sky

Daily Psalms and Directions of the Heart
for the Ten Days of Returning

חלון, ציפור, רקיע
שיר של יום וכוונת הלב
לעשרת ימי תשובה

Introduction

This section provides readings for the period of time from Rosh Hashanah to Yom Kippur.* The Daily Psalms offered here, along with the accompanying Directions of the Heart, are intended to support quiet openness and inner reflection.

The Daily Psalm, *Shir Shel Yom*—literally, "poem [or song] of the day"—borrows its name from one of the earliest elements of the morning service. In the time of the Temple, the Levites assigned each day of the week its own biblical psalm, imparting the weekdays with individual identities in the context of an otherwise uniform service. Similarly, in the sequence provided here, each of the Ten Days of Returning is given a lyric poem with a unique focus.

The Direction of the Heart, *Kavanat Haleyv*, derives its name and function from the rabbinic concept of "directing the heart" in prayer. For the rabbis of the Talmud, *kavanah*—literally, "direction" or "intention"—was an essential aspect of authentic praying. Although they saw a need for fixed elements in the liturgy, the rabbis considered a full engaging of heart and mind to be equally important.

In post-talmudic times, the word *kavanah* developed a second liturgical usage. The kabbalists composed introductory passages to highlight mystical meanings in the prayers, calling their compositions *kavanot* (plural of *kavanah*). The two meanings of *kavanah*—personal intentionality and a passage providing a focus for prayer—converge here in the genre of prose meditation: *kavanat haleyv*, "direction of the heart."

The sequence is preceded by an introductory meditation.

---

*The inclusion of special readings for the days between Rosh Hashanah and Yom Kippur takes as its precedent the *s'liḥot* prayers (petitions for forgiveness) that are traditionally recited daily during this period.

Meditation: Window, Bird, Sky

Birds, flying in and out of view. We see them, then we don't. We hear them singing or rustling the leaves; when we look for them, they are gone. They leave us for whole seasons — and then one day, we see they have returned. We didn't even know we were waiting.

Birds, flitting in and out, crossing the frames of the windows. Like everything else in our world — people, creatures, weeds in the yard — sometimes we feel their presence, sometimes not. Sometimes we feel their absence. Sometimes, not.

Sometimes we look out the window, sometimes we look in, sometimes we turn away. Always the sky holds all, subsumes all.

Window, bird, sky: perception, object, context. The whole of what is. To sit beside the window, immerse oneself in sky, let the birds swoop in and out of sight. Sometimes no birds come, but if we pay attention, we feel something stir.

At night, the window is a mirror. Phantom birds appear, real as the birds at noon. We are alone, but we are never alone.

The Gift

Sitting before a window, with no desire
but to see with the heart, clearly:

you watch the shadows come
and go,

you let yourself be forgiven.

Clouds cross the sky, mending
the roughened edges here and there,

partway through your life.

Seeing with the Heart

Windows invite us to see the world outside ourselves—
but not all seeing is the same. There is seeing with the eyes
and there is seeing with the mind. *Aha! I see*, we say when
we have an *insight*. We look back in *hindsight*, plan ahead
with *foresight*, keep things in order with *oversight*. When
we miss a step, we call that *oversight* too.

And there is a kind of seeing that we might call *undersight*.
Seeing under, beneath the surfaces; seeing into, through
and through; taking in the whole of what is. We might
also call this *heartsight*—seeing with the heart—because
seeing deeply renders us more understanding and
compassionate. Is it not easier to forgive when one sees
beyond the actions, sees through to the humanity, in all its
flaws and limitations, of someone who has caused us pain?

Birthday of the World

Today is the birthday of the world.
But the world knows nothing
of this invention.

The world just keeps moving about itself,
buzzing and humming, exulting and keening,
birthing and being born,

while the mind keeps on its own way —
form-craving, metaphor-making,
over and over, giving birth and being born.

Giving Birth

Hayom harat olam: *Today is the birthday of the world, the day on which the world was conceived* — so we say each Rosh Hashanah. And today it is being born again — as it is every day, at every hour. With each moment, the old world disappears and a new world comes into being. Everything always happening for the first time.

Why, then, is *this* birthday special? On Rosh Hashanah, we set out on a path of deliberate change, change that is in our own powers to effect — *t'shuvah*, the return to one's truest self.

As we celebrate the birthday of the world, the great creation out of which we are born, we bring attention to the ongoing creation of our lives, by which we make ourselves new each day.

Awakening

A sudden thud at the window
stops the morning
from veering off to a forgettable place.

Where were you before you looked up
to see the smashed feathers,
the smudge of blood on the pane?

Presence

We spend much of our waking time overtaken by busy-
ness, overwhelmed by the world roiling around us, pulled
in all directions at once. Yet we are also capable of being
focused, keenly alert and aware — present of mind and
heart.

Such presence may be brought upon us by a source
outside ourselves. We may be stunned into alertness by
a dramatic event — a birth, a death, a grievous loss — or
stirred to it by an encounter with beauty. At times we are
suddenly awakened by something small appearing in our
path — and at once, the world becomes new.

On days when nothing extraordinary seems to happen,
we have a chance to be more awake to ordinary moments.
Being present to the moment brings about a near-
magical transformation, by which ordinary life becomes
extraordinary.

Like Buds

Such gratitude as might be held
by the wide-spreading topmost branches

of the most noble trees —
Where can it go, if not up

to the heavens, or to the depths
of earth, which yields

to every step, commanding
nothing? Or perhaps

it has no destination, no reason
beyond itself for being —

like buds that cannot help but open,
never stop opening — Oh

what's the difference, what's
this need to know? Let it go

wherever, to burst the seams of meanness,
puncture the blistering regrets,

letting loose the grieving
to nowhere

or somewhere,
whether or not you know its name.

Gratitude

Gratitude: the gift one gives to oneself. Blessing of blessings, filling the heart, lifting us, softening us. Balm to our sorrows, salve to our wounds.

Many traditional blessings are prayers of gratitude to God. But one can also feel and express gratitude without directing it to a particular source. Gratitude can be experienced as a wholeness within the self that goes beyond the self: the self expanding into a great fullness — gratefulness.

But how can one feel grateful when one is suffering? How does one feel gratitude in the midst of grave illness or grief? Just seeing the suffering of others can bring one to despair.

Sometimes the feeling of gratefulness comes without effort — a kind of grace. At other times, one has to actively seek out the gifts, large or small, that have gone unnoticed.

It is said that the measure of one's happiness is one's gratitude. The practice of looking for the hidden gifts, within and outside oneself, can bring tranquility and joy, even in darker times.

Wind

It begins, you imagine,
as something captured —

a ball of blue atmosphere
or a pocket of darkness

pushing against its seams
until they split apart

and it rushes out in joy
to your window.

How the trees shake and sway,
letting loose their yellow, calling,

*Let go the wreath of sadness
crowning your head.*

Sadness

Sadness: the guest that comes unbidden and leaves in its own time. Its guises take many shapes and colors: grief's midnight indigo, sorrow's predawn gray. The searing red of sudden separation. And sometimes it is a colorless thing that visits for no apparent reason, quietly inhabiting one's cells, unremarkable as breathing.

At such times, relief may be sought in the world's large and small beauties: light shifting in the sky as the sun burns an opening in the clouds; jays calling to one another across a maze of high branches; the smell of rain on cut grass, narcissus in first bloom. Wind on your limbs as you walk the open field, kindness on a stranger's face as you pass her on the street.

As the self can be a refuge when you are world-weary, so the world can revive you when you are weary of yourself.

Step outside, let the world comfort you.

Morning *Minyan*

A quorum of small black birds
settles on the birch outside the window:

ten of them, enough to pray
the most sacred prayers.

Whom do they beseech,
for what do they pray

with their *too-too*s
and *dee-dee-dee*s?

Do they ask for grace?
Cannot be. They already have it.

Do they seek forgiveness? For what?
They cannot help but do what birds do.

Do they need healing?
Perhaps one of them has broken a wing?

Or are they singing praises of the Creator?
Of the creation? Of the many ilks and varieties of bird?

You would like to stay and find out,
but you have no time this morning.

No time no time no time no time
chants our species.

Dit-dit-dit, dit-dit-dit, dit-dit-dit-dit
cry the birds as they fly away.

Minyan: Traditionally, the minimum number of adults required for
communal recitation of certain prayers.

Time

We use it — wisely or not. We fill it and mark it. We try to stop it, but there is no end to it. And yet, we never have enough.

It is a circle, and it is a line. Moving forward, day by day, year by year, we come round and round again. Again the spring, again the fall — but every leaf a new one, every fall a new shape falling.

Always starting, never finished, we live always in the between.

No time, we say, we have no time. Yet we have all the time in the world.

And there is no time like now.

When You Look in the Mirror

Don't dwell on the fickleness of the past—
bring your thoughts to the one certain thing.

Think of it when you start to feel sorry
for yourself, and think of it

when you are happy: its dark flavor
will intensify your joy. Yes—

remember it as much as you can,
let yourself be filled with it.

And when you overhear the mustard weed
whisper to the vetch,

Yellow and purple, purple and yellow,
aren't we the beauties of the hill?

think how the snow will cover their traces,
and how dumb-lucky you are right now.

Death

It is everywhere, but when do we pay it attention? We see the bloom; do we notice the withered stalk? Where are the shrouds and burial sites? Who carries the roadkill away?

Look around, find it, peer into its face. The bloom will brighten, the birds will swoop into view.

Open Wings

If you draw a bird from her nest,
away from her elaborate labors,
seducing her with seed —

If you draw the curtains apart
so she sees your cupped hand
beckoning at the sill —

If you draw water to fill the stone bath
where she drinks and preens
and washes her wings —

when she comes, open-winged,
her throat filled with music,
will she bring you back to yourself?

Open Questions

Opening to the world, does the self open to itself? Or must the world be shut out to make room for the self to find its way?

Which came first — world or self? Which will be here last?

Do self and world need each other to exist? Are they separate or parts of a single whole? Or are they one and the same?

What are the questions we need to ask?

What are the questions we don't yet know to ask?

What Do You Hear?

A bird that calls
five calls
and waits for its mate.

A roar of distant traffic
or ocean
that turns out to be wind.

A caw like a door swinging open.

The foghorns warn without cease:
*Here is rock, here
is the edge.*

When the mate answers,
the bird calls again
five times.

The trees look too large to creak
but they do
because of the wind.

When the wind is up,
even the small grasses
find their low voice.

Nothing to be made
of any of it. No lessons
in the afternoon sounds.

Only the music
as the sounds drift apart
and float back together into silence.

Silence

What do we hear when we let it settle in us?

What Do You Have?

Not this earth, not even dust—
Not yours, caw invisible crows
like doors swinging shut.

Not your memories, rising
and burning in the air
like leaf-dew in sun.

Not your thoughts, poking in
and darting out
like hummingbirds among the blossoms.

Only this bit of time (like clouds unforming)—
even as you point to it,
gone.

Nothing

Nothing. You began as nothing and you will end as nothing. And in between — everything, and nothing. In between — joy and sorrow, beauty and decay. Everything yours to partake of, yours to bear. Yours to see, to know, to give birth to — and to let go. None of it yours to have.

Not even you are yours to have. You belong to a wholeness so great you cannot even conceive of it.

No, it is not a belonging; nothing owns you. You are simply part of it. You came out of it and you will return to it. You do not ever leave it, you are part of it forever.

And this is your moment to be alive.

Three ❦ Yom Kippur

יום הכיפורים

Gathering In

Yom Kippur Eve

♥

התכנסות

ליל הכיפורים

נטילת ידיים

אֶרְחַץ בְּנִקָּיוֹן כַּפָּי.
—תהלים כו, ו

תִּזְכֹּר נַפְשֵׁנוּ
אֶת קְדָשַׁת הַגּוּף
בִּנְטִילַת יָדָיִם.

Washing the Hands

I will wash my palms
in innocence.
—Psalms 26:6

Washing the hands,
we call to mind
the holiness of body.

The mealtime blessings—"Washing the Hands," "Blessing before the Meal," and "Blessing after the Meal"—are not actually part of Yom Kippur. They are provided here for *s'udah mafséket*, the meal eaten just before beginning the fast. There is no *kiddush* (blessing over wine); with the lighting of the candles, the fast begins.

ברכת הלחם

וְלֶחֶם לְבַב־אֱנוֹשׁ יִסְעָד.
—תהלים קד, טו

נְבָרֵךְ אֶת עֵין הַחַיִּים
הַמּוֹצִיאָה לֶחֶם מִן הָאָרֶץ.

Blessing before the Meal

Bread is the sustenance of the heart.
—Psalms 104:15

Let us bless the source of life
that brings forth bread from the earth.

ברכת המזון

וַאֲכַלְתֶּם לַחְמְכֶם לָשׂבַע
וִישַׁבְתֶּם לָבֶטַח בְּאַרְצְכֶם.
—ויקרא כו, ה

כִּי־יִהְיֶה בְךָ אֶבְיוֹן . . .
פָּתֹחַ תִּפְתַּח אֶת־יָדְךָ לוֹ.
—דברים טו, ז–ח

נוֹדֶה לְעֵין הַחַיִּים
הַזָּנָה אֶת הַכֹּל.

נִשְׁמֹר עַל הָאָרֶץ
הַטּוֹבָה וְהָרְחָבָה
וְהִיא תְּקַיְּמֵנוּ

וּנְבַקֵּשׁ שִׂבְעַת לֶחֶם
לְכָל הַדָּרִים בָּהּ.

Blessing after the Meal

You will eat your fill of bread
and dwell securely on the land.
—Leviticus 26:5

If there is a needy person among you . . .
open your hand and give.
—Deuteronomy 15:7–8

We are grateful for the riches
of the good, giving earth.

We will tend the earth's gifts,
that they may flourish,

and seek sustenance for all
who dwell here with us.

הדלקת נרות ותחילת הצום

הֲלוֹא זֶה צוֹם אֶבְחָרֵהוּ.

פַּתֵּחַ חַרְצֻבּוֹת רֶשַׁע,
הַתֵּר אֲגֻדּוֹת מוֹטָה

וְשַׁלַּח רְצוּצִים חָפְשִׁים
וְכָל־מוֹטָה תְּנַתֵּקוּ.

הֲלוֹא פָרֹס לָרָעֵב לַחְמֶךָ
וַעֲנִיִּים מְרוּדִים תָּבִיא בָיִת,

כִּי־תִרְאֶה עָרֹם וְכִסִּיתוֹ
וּמִבְּשָׂרְךָ לֹא תִתְעַלָּם.

אָז יִבָּקַע כַּשַּׁחַר אוֹרֶךָ
וַאֲרֻכָתְךָ מְהֵרָה תִצְמָח.
—ישעיה נח, ו–ח

תְּהֵא הַמַּחְשָׁבָה צְלוּלָה,
הַנֶּפֶשׁ רְווּיַת אוֹר

בִּשְׁעַת הַדְלָקַת נֵרוֹת
וְרֵאשִׁית הַצּוֹם
שֶׁל יוֹם הַכִּפּוּרִים.

Lighting the Candles, Beginning the Fast

This is the fast I choose:

To unlock the chains of evil
and untie the cords of enslavement,

to free the oppressed
and break off the yoke.

Share your bread with the hungry,
bring the poor into your home.

When you see the naked, clothe them,
and do not overlook your kin.

Then your light will break forth like the dawn
and your healing will rapidly blossom.
—Isaiah 58:6–8

May the mind be clear,
the spirit awake

as we light the candles
and begin.

On the eves of Sabbaths and holidays, it is customary to draw the light of the candles toward oneself with a gesture of the hands. On Yom Kippur — the last and most introspective day of the season — this gesture might express a gathering of focus and attention. Because there is no *kiddush* on Yom Kippur, the Blessing of Renewal ("*sheheḥeyánu*") follows upon candlelighting.

ברכת הזמן

הַמְשַׁלֵּחַ מַעְיָנִים בַּנְּחָלִים
בֵּין הָרִים יְהַלֵּכוּן.
—תהלים קד, י

נָבוֹא בַּשְּׁעָרִים, מוֹדִים
עַל חֶסֶד הַהִתְחַדְּשׁוּת.

נְבָרֵךְ אֶת מַעְיַן חַיֵּינוּ
שֶׁהֶחֱיָנוּ וְקִיְּמָנוּ וְהִגִּיעָנוּ
לַזְּמַן הַזֶּה.

Blessing of Renewal

Springs and rivers gush forth,
flowing between the hills.
— Psalms 104:10

We enter the gates, grateful
for the blessing of renewal.

Let us bless the flow of life
that revives us,
sustains us,
and brings us to this time.

ברכת הבת, ברכת הבן

וּרְחֹבוֹת הָעִיר יִמָּלְאוּ
יְלָדִים וִילָדוֹת
מְשַׂחֲקִים בִּרְחֹבֹתֶיהָ.
—זכריה ח, ה

ברכת הבת

[שם הילדה]—

הֱיִי אֲשֶׁר תִּהְיִי
וַהֲיִי בְּרוּכָה
בַּאֲשֶׁר תִּהְיִי.

❧

ברכת הבן

[שם הילד]—

הֱיֵה אֲשֶׁר תִּהְיֶה
וֶהֱיֵה בָּרוּךְ
בַּאֲשֶׁר תִּהְיֶה.

Blessing the Children

The squares of the city will be filled
with boys and girls playing.
—Zechariah 8:5

[The child's name] —

Be who you are,
and may you be blessed
in all that you are.

Turning the Heart

תשובת הלב

התעטפות בטלית

עֹטֶה־אוֹר כַּשַּׂלְמָה,
נוֹטֶה שָׁמַיִם כַּיְרִיעָה.
—תהלים קד, ב

כְּנָפַיִם פְּרוּשׂוֹת
יַעַטְפוּ אֶת הַגּוּף,
לֵב וָנֶפֶשׁ יַעֲטוּ אוֹר
בְּהִתְעַטְּפִי בַּטַּלִּית.

Tallit: Prayer Shawl

Wrapped in a robe of light,
spreading the skies like a canopy.
— Psalms 104:2

Enveloped in light, I wrap around me
the widespread wings of the *tallit*.

The *tallit* is customarily worn only during daytime services, except on
Yom Kippur, when it is worn also in the evening.

Introduction to *Kol Nidrey*: All Vows

Kol Nidrey, one of the most commented-upon and puzzled-over passages of the holiday liturgy, is not a prayer per se but a declaration annulling all oaths and vows. Nor is it actually part of the Yom Kippur evening service but, rather, a prelude to it. Although it was popularly embraced at the time of its composition, *Kol Nidrey* was the subject of rabbinic controversy and debate for centuries before becoming a firmly established part of the liturgy — and it has continued to be controversial since that time.

Contrary to a commonly held belief about its original raison d'être, *Kol Nidrey* was not created in reaction to forced conversions during the Spanish Inquisition (which began in the late fifteenth century). Although its origins are unclear, we know it to be at least as old as the ninth century. By the sixteenth century it had become a high point of the Ashkenazic liturgy, as a result of having been set to a hauntingly beautiful melody.

Kol Nidrey's original context was legalistic; rabbis did indeed annul certain vows. But *Kol Nidrey* also expressed spiritual feelings fitting for the High Holiday season: on Yom Kippur, individuals yearned to enter the new year with a clean slate, released from unfulfilled promises made to God. In its earliest version, *Kol Nidrey* referred to vows made in the preceding year; centuries later, it was revised by the rabbis to refer to vows to be made in the period "between this Yom Kippur and the next." In part, this change was intended to avoid the appearance of annulment of existing legal obligations between people.

Today, *Kol Nidrey* remains problematic for many rabbis and worshipers. Beyond questioning the moral validity of nullifying vows, one might ask what it actually *means* to vacate a *future* vow. If one nullifies a vow that one has not yet made, what does this do to the meaning of "vow" itself?

The re-creation offered here does not attempt to resolve the moral questions raised by the traditional formula. Rather, it recasts *Kol Nidrey* as a different kind of preparation for prayer: at the onset of Yom Kippur, we seek to be released from unfulfilled and unfulfilling expectations we have of ourselves so that we may be fully receptive to what unfolds.

Kol Nidrey is beloved today not so much for its meaning as for its melody: the words (which are not in Hebrew but in Aramaic) have become a structure on which to pin the musical notes. It would be unrealistic to expect this new passage to take the place of *Kol Nidrey*, nor is it intended to do so. Instead, it might serve as a recitation or meditation to precede or follow the singing of the traditional words.

כל נדרי

כָּל נֶדֶר, שְׁבוּעָה וְהַבְטָחָה
שֶׁנָּדַרְנוּ לְעַצְמֵנוּ
וְתַכְלִיתָם אָבְדָה—

לוּ תִּרְפֶּה אֲחִיזָתָם:

נִהְיֶה קַשּׁוּבִים
עַד תֹּם
לְכֹבֶד הַשָּׁעָה.

Kol Nidrey: All Vows

All vows —
all promises and pledges —

that we have made to ourselves
and that no longer serve
for the good —

may their grip be loosened

that we be present of mind and heart
to the urgency of the hour.

תשובת הלב

אילת השחר שבקע אורה . . .
כך היא גאולתם של ישראל:
בתחילה קמעא־קמעא,
כל מה שהיא הולכת
היא רבה והולכת.
—תלמוד ירושלמי ברכות, א, ה

סִיבוּב הָאֲדָמָה אִטִּי
אֶל מוּל שָׁמַיִם—

בִּלְתִּי מוּחָשׁ, אַךְ
יוֹצֵר יוֹם וְלַיְלָה.

אֶבֶן אַחַת מֻשְׁלֶכֶת
אֶל תּוֹךְ הַנַּחַל—

וְהַמַּיִם עוֹלִים
קִמְעָה קִמְעָה.

Turning the Heart

[Like] the morning star whose light bursts forth . . .
so Israel's redemption will come:
bit by bit at first,
bigger and bigger as it makes its way.
—Talmud (y. Berakhot 1:5)

Slow spin of earth
against sky—

imperceptible, yet
making the days.

One stone tossed
into the current,

and the river, ever-
so-slightly, rising.

וִדּוּי

עִמְדוּ עַל־דְּרָכִים וּרְאוּ
וְשַׁאֲלוּ לִנְתִבוֹת עוֹלָם
אֵי־זֶה דֶרֶךְ הַטּוֹב, וּלְכוּ־בָהּ
וּמִצְאוּ מַרְגּוֹעַ לְנַפְשְׁכֶם.
—ירמיה ו, טז

בְּמַרְאַת עֵינֵינוּ
מִשְׁתַּקֵּף הַזּוּלָת,

בְּמַרְאַת עֵינֵי הַזּוּלָת
נִגְלִים פָּנֵינוּ.

נַבִּיט פְּנִימָה, נִרְאֶה
אֵיךְ הִכְאַבְנוּ,

אֵיךְ לָן הַכְּאֵב
גַּם בְּפֶצַע קָטָן.

נִשְׁאַל עֲנָוָה
לְבַקֵּשׁ סְלִיחָה,

נִמְצָא מַרְגּוֹעַ
לְנַפְשֵׁנוּ.

Confession

Stand at the roads, and consider.
Look into the paths of the past,
see which is the road of goodness.
Walk it, and find tranquility.
—Jeremiah 6:16

In the mirror of our eyes,
the other is reflected;

in the eyes of the other—
ourselves.

We look outward,
inward,

see how we have hurt
and harmed,

how hurt embeds even
in the smallest wounds.

We give ourselves over,
begin to make amends,

begin
to make ourselves whole.

The traditional prayers of confession recited on Yom Kippur are lists,
in abecedarian form, of sins that may have been committed in the past
year by oneself or other members of the community. This re-creation
replaces that catalogue with a call to self-accounting.

ונתנה תוקף קדושת היום

ראו עמודים 28–35.

Un'taneh Tókef K'dushat Hayom:
We Declare the Utter Sanctity of This Day

See pages 28–35.

Remembering the Lives

(Yizkor Service)

הזכרת נשמות

Introduction

"Remembering the Lives" re-creates the memorial service commonly known as *Yizkor*—literally, "May God remember"—which takes place on Yom Kippur and on the "pilgrimage festivals" of Sukkot, Passover, and Shavu'ot. Although recited four times a year, *Yizkor* was original to Yom Kippur and only later added to the festival liturgies. And indeed, it feels especially appropriate to Yom Kippur, which focuses throughout on the place of death in our lives.

The core of the traditional *Yizkor* asks God to "remember the soul" of a deceased family member. Because of its personal nature, this petition, in contrast to most of the liturgy, is in the singular voice ("my mother" rather than "our mothers"). The re-creation is even more personal: it focuses on one's own recollection of the deceased. Thus it opens, in Hebrew, with the word *ezkor*, "I remember (or recall)."

In Reform and modern Conservative liturgies, the service begins with several verses from Psalms. These are followed by the petition and the whole of Psalm 23 ("The Lord is my shepherd, I shall not want . . ."), a quintessential prayer of comfort. The service closes with the mourner's *Kaddish*.

The re-creation is in four sections, each one parallel to a section of the service outlined above (though not presented in the same order): "I Recall," "Poems of Grief and Consolation," "Beneath Shekhinah's Wings," and "*Kaddish*: Beauty of the World."

The *Ezkor* recitation substitutes for the *Yizkor* petition.

---

*"Remembering the Lives" may also serve as an independent memorial ceremony at other times of the year.

Unlike the *Yizkor*, it allows the awareness that all lives are complex and feelings are rarely unalloyed. People close to us may, willingly or unwillingly, have caused us hurt or harm; "I Recall" offers a way to mourn while acknowledging the fullness of one's experience.

The sequence "Poems of Grief and Consolation" takes the place of verses from the Psalms. Its seven poems (the number echoes the seven days of *shivah*, the initial stage of mourning after a burial) form a progression from initial shock and grief ("Before and After," "Grief's House"), to consolation and healing ("Birds in a Dying Birch," "Enduring," "Another View"), to acceptance of death and recognition of one's own mortality ("Earth," "You Do Not Belong to You"). The poems are introduced with a seven-part meditation, "Passageways of Grieving."

"Beneath Shekhinah's Wings" parallels Psalm 23 in purpose. Shekhinah (the Hebrew word means "indwelling") is a traditional name for divine presence, associated with comfort and protection. The phrase *táḥat kan'fey hash'khinah*, "beneath Shekhinah's wings," is from a hymn customarily recited at funerals, *El Maley Raḥamim*, "God of Compassion."

"*Kaddish*: Beauty of the World," is an exhortation to praise. It takes its theme from the traditional *Kaddish*, which is a paean to the glory of God.

אזכור

לזכר נשמות שנגעו בחיי

אַעֲלֶה עַל לִבִּי
אֶת רִקְמַת חַיֶּיהָ/חַיָּיו:

מַרְאוֹת גּוֹאִים
וּנְמוֹגִים,

רְגָעִים
מִתּוֹךְ שֶׁטֶף הַזְּמַן—

עֲנָגִים, קָשִׁים,
מַרְנִינִים, פּוֹגְעִים—

לוּ יִהְיוּ נִימֵי הַזִּכְרוֹנוֹת
שְׁזוּרִים בְּמַאֲרַג חַיַּי

לָרֻפָּא.

I Recall

In memory of lives that touched one's own

I call her/him to mind and heart,
the texture of her/his life,
its presence in mine.

Images rise up
and fall away,
moments in the current of time —

tender, harsh,
extraordinary,
mundane,

that which gives pleasure in recollection
and that which hurts, yet resists
being forgotten.

May the threads of memory be woven
into the fabric of my life
and bring healing.

כוונות לשעת אבל

הלם. גם כשנדמהֶ שאנו מוכנים, מות יקירינו מגיע אלינו כהלם. העולם הופך לאחר, וצריך ללמוד, כמו בראשונה, לחיות.

❧

הזיכרונות—כמו מבקרים הבאים והולכים בשבעה. מחזיקים בנו—ומניחים לנו ללכת.

❧

משהו קטן ויפהפה מופיע, ממלא פיסה של חלל ריק שנותר, בור בלב שלא נאטם. רגע ראשון, אולי, של ריפוי.

❧

אנו דוחים את האפשרות שאבלנו יקטן; אנו חשים שזו בגידה: כל עוד מתגעגעים אליהם, הם נוכחים. אך החיים יודעים שהזמן לא ישוב לאחור, שכל הדברים משתנים. אפילו הצער, אפילו האבל.

❧

יש נחמה בתחושה שאנו חלק מן העולם—עולם הטבע, עולם אדם. הבידוד החריף של האבל נכנע לזיכרון ישָׁן: איננו לבד.

❧

Passageways of Grieving

Shock. Even when you think you are prepared, it comes as a shock. There was one world before — and another world after. And you must learn, as for the first time, how to live in the world.

❧

They move from room to room, the memories — like visitors entering and leaving the house of *shivah*, where the bereaved sit in mourning. Coming and going, coming and going. Holding on, and letting go.

❧

Something small and beautiful appears, filling part of the vacuum that has been left, the hole in your heart that hasn't closed. The first moment, perhaps, of healing.

❧

You resist believing your grief will diminish, because that belief feels like a betrayal: as long as you go on missing them, they are present. But life carries within itself the knowledge that time will not be undone, that all things change with time. Even your sorrow, even your grief.

❧

The solace of feeling yourself part of the world again — the natural world, the human world. The intense isolation of grief succumbs to an older memory: you are not alone.

❧

ניתן למצוא מרגוע בחופן עפר שהתחמם בשמש, ממש
כמו ההבנה שאנו הולכים ומתים מן הרגע בו נולדנו.

❦

התרוממות: הידיעה שאנו חלק מהסוד. הבינה והלב
נכנעים: אנו מניחים לעצמנו להילקח.

There comes the knowledge that we are, all of us, always dying. From the moment of birth, dying back into the world, out of which we were born.

❧

A lifting: the awareness that one is part of the mystery. Mind and heart surrender. You let yourself be taken.

שִׁירֵי אֵבֶל וְנֶחָמָה

לִפְנֵי וְאַחֲרֵי

עֲנָנִים גּוֹעֲשִׁים בִּשְׁחָקִים אַדִּירִים,
צַפְצָפוֹת מְפִיצוֹת עֲלֵיהֶן בָּרוּחַ—

הוֹ אֵיךְ דְּבָרִים נִסְחָפִים וְאֵינָם
לְעֵינֵי הָעוֹמֶדֶת שָׁם אֵין־אוֹנִים,

מַבִּיטָה בַּמָּטָר דֶּרֶךְ כְּתָב שֶׁל עֵצִים
כַּאֲשֶׁר צִפּוֹר קְטַנָּה, נוֹצוֹתֶיהָ קַלּוֹת,

נוֹגַעַת בִּפְנֵי הַסְּלָעִים,
וּמַמְרִיאָה שׁוּב לַחָפְשִׁי.

וְעַכְשָׁו עוֹד אַחַת, דַּקַּת־גֵּו וּלְבָנָה,
מַמְרִיאָה בְּאוֹתָהּ הַקֶּשֶׁת,

עֵינָהּ הַבְּהִירָה, הַכָּחֻלָּה
זוֹהֶרֶת לִפְנֵי הָעָלְמָה.

Before and After

Clouds erupt in the enormous sky,
poplars fling their leaves into the wind —

Oh how a thing is swept away
as one stands there, helpless,

watching the rain through a calligraphy of trees
while a small, light-feathered bird

skims the surface of the rocks,
then swoops up again and flies free.

Now another — white-winged and slender —
takes the same arc,

its clear, aquamarine eye flashing a brilliant light
before it is gone.

בֵּית אֵבֶל

דֶּלֶת אַחַר דֶּלֶת
נִפְתַּחַת, נִסְגֶּרֶת;
בָּזוֹ אַחַר זוֹ
אַתְּ נִכְנֶסֶת וְיוֹצֵאת.

וְרָדִים עַל אַבְנֵי הַקִּיר
מַתִּירִים לְחָנִים אֲפֵלִים
אֶל חֲלַל הָאֲוִיר
הָאוֹסֵף כָּל צְלִיל אֶל חֵיקוֹ
וְשׁוֹלֵחַ אוֹתוֹ לְדַרְכּוֹ.

חוּטֵי עָלִים חֲדָשִׁים
נִתְלִים מֵאֲמִיר הַלִּבְנֶה
כִּשְׂעָרוֹת בָּרוּחַ
פְּרוּעוֹת, לֹא סֹרָקוּ

וְהַבּוּגֶנְוִילֵיאָה
מַתִּיזָה אָדֹם עַל הַחַלּוֹן,
שׁוֹבֶרֶת אֶת לִבֵּךְ בִּגְלַל
מָה שֶׁאֵינֵךְ יְכוֹלָה לִשְׁכֹּחַ.

Grief's House

Door after door
opens and shuts;
one by one
you enter and leave.

Roses on the outer walls
release their dark music into the air,
which accepts each note completely
before letting it go.

Threads of new leaves
suspended from the top of the birch
sway in the wind like hair
let loose to be brushed

and the bougainvillea
splatters its red on the window,
breaking your heart because of all
you cannot help but remember.

צִפּוֹרִים עַל צַפְצָפָה גּוֹסֶסֶת

לוּלֵי מִסְפָּרָם
יְכוֹלָה הָיִית שֶׁלֹא לִרְאוֹתָם:
זַהֲבָנִים צְהֻבֵּי בֶּטֶן, רַבִּים מִסְפֹּר,
נֶאֶסְפוּ עַל רוּם צַמַּרְתּוֹ שֶׁל הָעֵץ הָעֵירֹם.

פִּיצוּי? אוֹ רַק נֶחָמָה?
פִּיצוּץ הַצֶּבַע הַזֶּה, שֶׁמַּתְרִיס בְּךָ
לֹא לְהַבִּיט לְאָחוֹר.

Birds in a Dying Birch

But for their numbers, you might miss them:
yellow-bellied warblers, too many to be counted,
gathering in the topmost branches of the naked tree.

Is it recompense, or merely consolation —
this burst of color, daring you
not to look back?

לָשֵׂאת

כְּמוֹ לְהִתְעוֹרֵר אַחֲרֵי מַחֲלָה אֲרֻכָּה
לִמְצֹא שֶׁבְּרִיאוּתְךָ שָׁבָה בִּשְׁנָתְךָ,
צַעַרְךָ יָסֹג בְּבוֹא זְמַנּוֹ
וְהַדַּעַת שֶׁנָּשָׂאתָ לְאֹרֶךְ חַיֶּיךָ
תַּחֲזֹר וְתוֹפִיעַ, שְׁלֵמָה וּבָרָה.

יוֹם אֶחָד לֹא תַּחְבֹּט עוֹד
בָּאוֹר הַבָּהִיר מִנְּשֹׂא,
לֹא תָּתוּר אַחַר קֶרֶן זָוִית
לַעֲצֹם שָׁם אֶת עֵינֶיךָ.
בֹּקֶר אֶחָד תֵּעוֹר
וְלֹא יִכְבְּדוּ עַפְעַפֶּיךָ
וְעַל לְשׁוֹנְךָ לֹא יִשְׁכֹּן
גּוּשׁ שֶׁל מֶלַח.

וּמִפְּנֵי שֶׁנּוֹתַרְתָּ זְמַן רַב
בְּלִי לְוַתֵּר,
בְּעוֹלָם שֶׁאֵינוֹ מְוַתֵּר,
תֵּדַע שֶׁהַזְּמַן עִקֵּשׁ,
שׂוֹרֶה וְיָכוֹל לָאֵבֶל

וְשֶׁכָּל הַדְּבָרִים נוֹלָדִים קְטַנִּים
וְהוֹלְכִים וּגְדֵלִים,
רַק הָאֵבֶל נוֹלָד גָּדוֹל
אַךְ הוֹלֵךְ וּפוֹחֵת.

Enduring

Like awakening after a long illness
to find your health stole back in while you slept,
your sorrow, in its time, will retreat,
and the knowledge you carried all along
will re-emerge, whole and cleansed.

One day you will not thrash in the too-bright light,
looking for a corner in which to close your eyes.
One morning the weight will not be there
beneath your eyelids, the first thing you wake to;
it will not settle on your tongue like a lump of salt.

And because you have stayed this long
unrelenting, in the unrelenting world,
you know that time, though imperfect,
is diligent, and wrestles down grief,

and that all things are born small
and grow large —
except grief, which is born large
and grows small.

מַרְאֶה אַחֵר

יוֹשֶׁבֶת בַּנֻּקְדָּה הַקְּבוּעָה מִתַּחַת לְעֵץ הַפִּלְפֵּל,
בְּצֵל עָמֹק עַד כִּי עַצְמוֹתַיִךְ נַעֲשׂוֹת כֹּה קָרוֹת
שֶׁעָלַיִךְ לָזוּז לַקָּצֶה הָרָחוֹק שֶׁל הַגַּן
שָׁם קַרְנֵי שֶׁמֶשׁ חַלָּשׁוֹת דּוֹלְפוֹת
מִבַּעַד לַפְּרִיחָה הַמְּאֻחֶרֶת—

מִשָּׁם תִּרְאִי אֶת הָעֵבֶר הַשֵּׁנִי שֶׁל הַדְּשָׁאִים
שֶׁאֶת צִבְעֵיהֶם וְצוּרָתָם חָשַׁבְתְּ שֶׁאַתְּ מַכִּירָה:
תִּרְאִי אֶת הַקְּצָווֹת הַחוּמִים הַמְּקֻרְזָלִים שֶׁל חֲבַצָּלוֹת הַקָּאלוֹת,
אֶת הַחֲרַקִּים הָאֲפֹרִים הַמִּתְגּוֹרְרִים בִּגְבִיעֵיהֶן,
אֶת הַחֶלְזוֹנוֹת הַנִּדְבָּקִים לְבִטְנוֹתֵיהֶן.

אַתְּ מְרִיצָה אֶת אֶצְבְּעוֹתַיִךְ לְאֹרֶךְ זַלְזַלֵּי הָאֶדֶר
שֶׁעֲלֵיהֶם הַמְּאֻדָּמִים יָבְשׁוּ וְהָפְכוּ לְתַחֲרָה שְׁבִירָה
הַנּוֹפֶלֶת אֶל יָדַיִךְ כְּשֶׁאַתְּ מְלַטֶּפֶת אוֹתָהּ.

פִּתְאֹם גִּבְעוֹלֵי הַקָּאלוֹת נִדְלָקִים כְּמוֹ נֵרוֹת
וְהַכֹּל נִרְאֶה לָעַיִן.

אָז אַתְּ חֲדֵלָה לַחֲשֹׁב עַל הַקֹּר
וְתוֹהָה לְאָן הוֹלֵךְ לוֹ הַיּוֹם
וְכַמָּה מֵעַצְמֵךְ יֵלֵךְ אִתּוֹ.

Another View

Sitting in your usual spot under the pepper tree,
in deep shade, until your bones become so cold
you have to move to the far end of the garden
where bits of sun leak
through the late-season blossoms —

From there you see the other side of grasses
whose colors and shapes you thought you knew:
you see the curled brown edges of the calla lilies,
the gray insects lodged in their cups,
the snails clinging to the undersides.

You run your fingers along the length of the maple twigs
whose reddened leaves have dried to a brittle lace
that falls into your hands as you stroke it.

Suddenly the lily stalks light up like candles
and everything is visible.

Then you stop thinking of cold
and wonder where the day is going
and how much of yourself will go along.

אֲדָמָה

אָהַבְתִּי אֵיךְ תִּפֹּל בְּלִי לְמַהֵר
בֵּין אֶצְבְּעוֹת יָדַי,
מוֹתִירָה סִימָנִים—

עֵץ וְחַמְצָה, פְּרִיחָה וּמַתֶּכֶת
בְּקִמְטֵי הָאֶצְבַּע,
בְּסַהֲרוֹן הַצִּפֹּרֶן;

אָהַבְתִּי אֵיךְ תָּנִיחַ בְּיָדִי אֶת מִשְׁקָלָהּ
כַּאֲשֶׁר חָפַרְתִּי בְּחֶשְׁכָּתָהּ,
וְאָנוּ אַחַת, אֵם וּבִתָּהּ;

וְאֵיךְ, כַּאֲשֶׁר אֲנִי שָׁבָה וּמַנִּיחָה אוֹתָהּ
סְבִיב שָׁרָשִׁים שֶׁנִּשְׁתְּלוּ זֶה עַתָּה
וְטוֹפַחַת עָלֶיהָ בְּכָרִיּוֹת יָדַי,

הִיא עוֹזֶבֶת אוֹתִי בְּלֹא הִתְנַגְּדוּת—
כְּדֶרֶךְ שֶׁשֵּׂעָר, עוֹר, רְאוּת וּבִינָה
נוֹטְשִׁים בְּשֶׁקֶט, תָּא אַחַר תָּא,

כָּל־כָּךְ בְּרֹךְ עַד כִּי לֹא אוּכַל לְדַמְיֵן
לְאֵיזוֹ מִטָּה רַכָּה, לְאֵיזֶה גוּף
אֲנִי נוֹלֶדֶת.

Earth

I like how it falls,
unhurried, between my fingers,
leaving traces of itself in the creases,

wood and acid,
flower and metal
in the crescents of the nails;

I like how, when I dig in its darkness,
it settles its weight in my hand,
at home with its child,

and how, when I lay it back
around the newly planted roots,
patting it down with the flat of my palm,

it leaves me again, without resisting.
The way hair, skin, sight, mind
go, quietly, cell by cell,

so gently I can only imagine
to what soft bed, what body
I am being delivered.

שירי אבל ונחמה

אֵינְךָ שַׁיָּךְ לְךָ

אַתָּה שַׁיָּךְ לַתֵּבֵל
וְתִדָּרֵשׁ בַּחֲזָרָה

מִטַּעַם לִבָּהּ הַנָּכוֹן
הַמִּשְׁתַּנֶּה לָעַד—

יְדָרְשׁוּ גוּפְךָ הֶחָכָם
וּבִינָתְךָ רַחֲבַת הַיָּדַיִם,

אִם לִבְּךָ רָחָב,
אִם לָאו,

אִם אַתָּה מוּכָן,
אִם לָאו,

אֲפִלּוּ כְּשֶׁאַתָּה פּוֹנֶה וְהוֹלֵךְ—
נֶחְבָּט

וְנִשָּׂא אֶל עַל,
זַלְזַל בָּרוּחַ.

You Do Not Belong to You

You belong to the universe
and you will be reclaimed

by its constant,
ever-changing heart —

your wise body
and your spacious mind,

when you are joyful
or not,

whether you are ready
or not,

even as you turn away —
to be buffeted

and set aloft,
a twig in the wind.

תחת כנפי השכינה

כְּנֶשֶׁר יָעִיר קִנּוֹ
עַל־גּוֹזָלָיו יְרַחֵף
יִפְרֹשׂ כְּנָפָיו יִקָּחֵהוּ,
יִשָּׂאֵהוּ עַל־אֶבְרָתוֹ.
—דברים לב, יא

הִיא מְרַחֶפֶת מֵעָלֵינוּ—
גּוֹזָלִים נְטוּשִׁים,
שְׁבוּרֵי לֵב—
וְנוֹשֵׂאת אֶת יְגוֹנֵנוּ.

בְּצֵל כְּנָפֶיהָ—
בַּיִת.

Beneath Shekhinah's Wings

Like an eagle stirring its nest,
hovering over its young,
taking them up on widespread wings,
lifting them to its breast.
 —Deuteronomy 32:11

She hovers over us,
her fledglings —

the bereaved,
the brokenhearted —

lifts us to her,
takes our sorrow.

In the depth of her shade:
home.

קדיש: יפעת תבל

הַלְלוּ אֶת הַתֵּבֵל,
הַלְלוּ אֶת מְלוֹאָה.

הַלְלוּ אֶת כְּסוּפֶיהָ,
אֶת יָפְיָה וִיגוֹנָה.

הַלְלוּ אֶבֶן וָאֵשׁ,
נָהָר וְלֵילָךְ

וְצִפּוֹר בּוֹדֵדָה
בַּחַלּוֹן.

הַלְלוּ אֶת רֶגַע
פְּרִיצַת הַשַּׁלֵם

וְאֶת רֶגַע פְּרִיצַת
הַשָּׁלֵם בְּרִנָּה.

הַלְלוּ בְּכָל מְאוֹדְכֶם
אֶת הַיֹּפִי הַדּוֹעֵךְ — וּרְאוּ

כִּי יִפְעַת הַתֵּבֵל
הִיא לָכֶם.

Kaddish: Beauty of the World

Praise the world —
praise its fullness

and its longing,
its beauty and its grief.

Praise stone and fire,
lilac and river,

and the solitary bird
at the window.

Praise the moment
when the whole
bursts through pain

and the moment
when the whole
bursts forth in joy.

Praise the dying beauty
with all your breath,
and praising, see

the beauty of the world
is your own.

N'ilah: Closing of the Gates

🍂

בעת נעילת שער

שעת נעילה

יִפָּתַח הַלֵּב
בְּעֵת נְעִילָתוֹ
כִּי פָנָה הַיּוֹם.

הַיּוֹם יִפְנֶה,
הַשֶּׁמֶשׁ יָבוֹא וְיִפְנֶה

וְקוֹל דְּמָמָה דַּקָּה
יְמַלֵּא אֶת הָאֲוִיר—

קוֹלוֹ שֶׁל הַלֵּב הַנִּשְׁבָּר,
קוֹלוֹ שֶׁל הַלֵּב
הַנִּפְתָּח.

Closing Hour

May the heart open
even in the hour of its closing
for the day draws to an end.

The day turns, the sun turns away,
and a voice of slender silence
rends the air —

sound of a breaking heart,
sound of the heart
breaking open.

The closing of the gates is a central metaphor of the *N'ilah* ("locking") service, which concludes Yom Kippur; it recalls the literal locking of the Temple gates at the end of every day. At the close of *N'ilah*, the metaphorical gates are said to be locked, sealing one's fate for the coming year. However, rabbinic teaching also maintains that one always has a chance to do *t'shuvah*; in this sense, the gates are never "locked." The first four lines of this re-creation parallel the language of one of the traditional *N'ilah* prayers. The last stanza turns the image of locking on its head.

N'ilah: Closing of the Gates

תקיעה גדולה

שְׁמַע, יִשְׂרָאֵל,
תְּקִיעָה גְּדוֹלָה:

הַקְּדֻשָּׁה שׁוֹפַעַת בַּכֹּל,
אַלְפֵי רְבָבָה פָּנֶיהָ,
מְלֹא עוֹלָם שְׁכִינָתָהּ.

הַכֹּל אֶחָד.
—בעקבות דברים ו, ד

The Great Call

Hear, O Israel,
the call of the shofar—

The divine abounds everywhere
and dwells in everything.

Its faces are infinite,
its source suffuses all.

The many are One.

Yom Kippur ends with the recitation of the *Sh'ma* (Deuteronomy 6:4), Judaism's declaration of monotheistic faith. The *Sh'ma* is re-visioned here (and in *Malkhuyot*, pages 42–45) as an affirmation of the unity of creation. It is followed by *t'kiah g'dolah*, the long final sounding of the shofar.

From End to Beginning

מאחרית לראשית

סיום הצום, ברכת הלחם

הֲלוֹא פָרֹס לָרָעֵב לַחְמֶךָ
וַעֲנִיִּים מְרוּדִים תָּבִיא בָיִת.
—ישעיה נח, ז

בְּתֹם הַצּוֹם נִזְכֹּר
אֶת הָרְעֵבִים לַלֶּחֶם.

נְבָרֵךְ אֶת עֵין הַחַיִּים
הַמּוֹצִיאָה לֶחֶם מִן הָאָרֶץ.

Breaking the Fast

Share your bread with the hungry
and bring the poor into your home.
—Isaiah 58:7

As we end the fast, we remember
those who hunger for bread.

Let us bless the source of life
that brings forth bread from the earth.

חתימה: שער פתוח

קֶשֶׁת הָעֶרֶב
עוֹלָה לְאַט,

צִלְלֵי חַמָּה כְּחֻלִּים
נִשְׁטָפִים, נְמוֹגִים.

הַשַּׁעַר עוֹדֶנּוּ פָּתוּחַ

עֵת שְׁלֹשָׁה כּוֹכָבִים
מַמְתִּינִים

לְפַלֵּחַ אֶת הָרָקִיעַ.

עֵת הַלַּיְלָה
חוֹשֵׂף אֶת מְבוֹכוֹ

שׁוּב נַתְחִיל
מִבְּרֵאשִׁית.

Coda: Open Gate

The arc of evening
slowly rising,

the sun's blue shadows
washed away,

the gate still open
as three stars

pierce the sky —
In the corridor

where night
bares its maze

we begin
to begin again.

Four 🖤 Entering the Gates

כניסה בשערים

תפילה לימים הנוראים

*באנגלית

Service for the High Holidays

This service is composed of elements from the first three parts of the book, arranged into a structured sequence for use as an alternative to traditional synagogue services. Except where indicated, each element is appropriate for both Rosh Hashanah and Yom Kippur. The shofar is sounded on Rosh Hashanah, after *Shofarot*, after *Zikhronot*, and after *Malkhuyot*.

*English only

התעטפות בטלית

עֹטֶה־אוֹר כַּשַּׂלְמָה,
נוֹטֶה שָׁמַיִם כַּיְרִיעָה.
—תהלים קד, ב

כְּנָפַיִם פְּרוּשׂוֹת
יַעַטְפוּ אֶת הַגּוּף,
לֵב וָנֶפֶשׁ יַעְטוּ אוֹר
בְּהִתְעַטְּפִי בַּטַּלִּית.

Tallit: Prayer Shawl

Wrapped in a robe of light,
spreading the skies like a canopy.
— Psalms 104:2

Enveloped in light, I wrap around me
the widespread wings of the *tallit*.

The *tallit* is customarily worn only during daytime services, except on
Yom Kippur, when it is worn also in the evening.

Service for the High Holidays

Birthday of the World

Today is the birthday of the world.
But the world knows nothing
of this invention.

The world just keeps moving about itself,
buzzing and humming, exulting and keening,
birthing and being born,

while the mind keeps on its own way—
form-craving, metaphor-making,
over and over, giving birth and being born.

Giving Birth

Hayom harat olam: Today is the birthday of the world, the day on which the world was conceived — so we say each Rosh Hashanah. And today it is being born again — as it is every day, at every hour. With each moment, the old world disappears and a new world comes into being. Everything always happening for the first time.

Why, then, is *this* birthday special? On Rosh Hashanah, we set out on a path of deliberate change, change that is in our own powers to effect — *t'shuvah*, the return to one's truest self.

As we celebrate the birthday of the world, the great creation out of which we are born, we bring attention to the ongoing creation of our lives, by which we make ourselves new each day.

פְּתִיחַת הַלֵּב

לִתְשׁוּבַת הַשָּׁנָה
בַּיָּמִים שֶׁבֵּין לְבֵין
נִפְנֶה עֹרֶף לַיָּדוּעַ

חַלּוֹן וְחָצֵר
גַּג וְגָדֵר

וְנִפְסַע בִּשְׁבִילִים
שֶׁטֶּרֶם נִתַּן
לְקָרְאָם בְּשֵׁם.

עָנָן וְשָׁמַיִם
עֲרִיפִים וּכְנָפַיִם

אַט אַט
יִפָּרְמוּ הַתְּפָרִים,
הַקָּשֶׁה יֵרֵךְ

סוּף וְשִׂיחַ
נַחַל וְרוּחַ

וְלֵב סָגוּר יִפָּתַח
לִסְלִיחָה.

Opening the Heart

At the year's turn,
in the days between

we step away
from what we know

> *wall and window*
> *roof and road*

into the spaces
we cannot yet name

> *cloud and sky*
> *cloud and wings*

Slowly the edges
begin to yield

the hard places
soften

> *wind and clover*
> *reed and river*

The gate to forgiveness
opens

ונתנה תוקף קדושת היום

וּנְתַנֶּה תֹּקֶף קְדֻשַּׁת הַיּוֹם
כִּי הוּא נוֹרָא וְאָיֹם.

וּבְשׁוֹפָר גָּדוֹל יִתָּקַע
וְקוֹל דְּמָמָה דַּקָּה יִשָּׁמַע.

קוֹל אֱנוֹשׁ—
קָנֶה בְּיַם הַסּוּף,
נְשׁיפָה בָּרוּחַ.

       ✦

בְּרֹאשׁ הַשָּׁנָה יִכָּתֵבוּן
וּבְיוֹם צוֹם כִּפּוּר יֵחָתֵמוּן.

חַיֵּינוּ סְפוּרִים
חֲקוּקִים בַּזְּמַן.

בִּתְשׁוּבַת הַשָּׁנָה
נַבִּיט קֶדֶם וְאָחוֹר,

נִזְכֹּר כִּי כָּל יָמֵינוּ
יָמִים שֶׁבֵּין לְבֵין:

Un'taneh Tókef K'dushat Hayom:
We Declare the Utter Sanctity of This Day

Un'taneh tókef k'dushat hayom
ki hu nora v'ayom.

Uv'shofar gadol yitaka
v'kol d'mamah dakah yishama.

We declare the utter sanctity of this day
for it is an awe-filled day.

A great shofar is sounded
and a voice of slender silence is heard.

> The voice is one's own —
> a reed in the chorus,
> a breath in the wind.

❧

B'rosh hashanah yikateyvun
uv'yom tzom kipur yeyḥateymun.

On Rosh Hashanah it is written
and on Yom Kippur it is sealed.

> Our lives are stories
> inscribed in time.
>
> At the turning of the year
> we look back, look ahead, see
>
> that we are always
> in the days between:

כַּמָּה יַעַבֹרוּן וְכַמָּה יִבָּרֵאוּן,
מִי יִחְיֶה וּמִי יָמוּת,
מִי בְקִצּוֹ וּמִי לֹא בְקִצּוֹ,
מִי בַמַּיִם וּמִי בָאֵשׁ,
מִי בַחֶרֶב וּמִי בַחַיָּה,
מִי בָרָעָב וּמִי בַצָּמָא,
מִי בָרַעַשׁ וּמִי בַמַּגֵּפָה,
מִי בַחֲנִיקָה וּמִי בַסְּקִילָה,
מִי יָנוּחַ וּמִי יָנוּעַ,
מִי יִשָּׁקֵט וּמִי יִטָּרֵף
מִי יִשָּׁלֵו וּמִי יִתְיַסָּר,
מִי יָרוּם וּמִי יֵשָׁפָל,
מִי יַעֲשִׁיר וּמִי יַעֲנִי.

❧

וּתְשׁוּבָה
וּתְפִלָּה
וּצְדָקָה
מַעֲבִירִין אֶת־רֹעַ הַגְּזֵרָה.

How many will leave this life
and how many will be born into it,
who will live and who will die,
whose life will reach its natural end
and whose will be cut short,
who by water and who by fire,
who by sword and who by beast,
who by hunger and who by thirst,
who by quake and who by plague,
who by choking and who by stoning,
who will rest and who will wander,
who will be tranquil and who will be torn,
who will be at peace and who will be tormented,
who will be raised high and who will be brought low,
who will prosper and who will be impoverished.

Ut'shuvah
Turning inward
to face one's self

Ut'filah
Entering into prayer
and contemplation

Utz'dakah
Giving to the needy,
as justice requires

Ma'avirin et-ró'a hag'zerah
These diminish the harshness
of the decree

וּתְשׁוּבָה

לָשׁוּב אֶל לִבַּת הַיְצִירָה
הַצָּרָה צוּרָה
לְכָל חַי וָחָי,

וּתְפִלָּה

לְהִתְעוֹרֵר אֶל זְרִימָה
שֶׁאֵינָהּ פּוֹסֶקֶת
בְּתוֹכֵנוּ וּסְבִיבֵנוּ,

לַחֲבֹק אֶת הַיֹּפִי הַחוֹלֵף,

וּצְדָקָה

לָדַעַת כִּי אָנוּ כֻּלָּנוּ
בָּשָׂר וָדָם
וְחַיֵּינוּ אֲרוּגִים—
מָתוֹק וּמַר,
מַר וּמָלוּחַ—

וּפְרִי הַחֶסֶד
חֶסֶד,
וּמַעֲשִׂים טוֹבִים
פָּעֳלוֹ,

מַעֲבִירִין אֶת־רֹעַ הַגְּזֵרָה.

נִתְבָּרֵךְ בְּעֹשֶׁר חַיֵּינוּ,
נִגְבַּר עַל אֵימַת הֶעָתִיד.

Ut'shuvah
>Returning to the inner artistry
>that gives each life its form,
>
>seeking to become
>one's truest self

Ut'filah
>Being alive to the unending flow
>within and around us,
>
>holding dear
>the transient beauty

Utz'dakah
>Knowing that we are, all of us,
>flesh and blood
>
>and our fates are intertwined —
>sweet with bitter, bitter with salt —
>
>and that the fruit of kindness
>is kindness,
>
>and good deeds
>are its fulfillment

Ma'avirin et-ró'a hag'zerah
>We become present
>to the fullness of our lives
>
>and untether ourselves from the fear
>of what lies ahead

יְסוֹדֵנוּ מֵעָפָר וְסוֹפֵנוּ לֶעָפָר.
בְּנַפְשֵׁנוּ נָבִיא לַחְמֵנוּ.

אָנוּ מְשׁוּלִים כַּחֶרֶס הַנִּשְׁבָּר,
כֶּחָצִיר יָבֵשׁ וּכְצִיץ נוֹבֵל,
כְּצֵל עוֹבֵר וּכְעָנָן כָּלֶה
וּכְרוּחַ נוֹשָׁבֶת וּכְאָבָק פּוֹרֵחַ
וְכַחֲלוֹם יָעוּף.

נוֹלַדְנוּ לַבְּרִיאָה
הַנּוֹשֵׂאת אוֹתָנוּ בְּחֵיקָהּ
וּבְחִבּוּקָהּ נָמוּת.

הַשָּׁלֵם יִכּוֹן לָעַד:
אֵין קֵץ לַנִּסְתָּר בּוֹ,
אֵין שִׁעוּר לְגִלּוּיָּיו,
אֵין קִצְבָּה לְשָׁנוֹתָיו.

גַּם בְּמוֹתֵנוּ
יִזָּכְרוּ כָּל שְׁמוֹתֵינוּ
בַּשָּׁלֵם הַגָּדוֹל.

וּנְתַנֶּה תֹקֶף קְדֻשַּׁת הַיּוֹם.

We begin in earth
and we end in earth.
We spend our lives earning our bread.
We are like broken vessels,
dry grass, withering blossoms,
passing shadows, vanishing clouds,
drifting wind, scattering dust,
a fleeting dream.

> Born in nature
> and borne by nature,
> we die in its lap-and-fold.

> The whole lives on,
> infinite in mystery,
> its manifestations numberless.

> Seeing beyond our separate deaths,
> we find our selves in the greater whole,
> our names embedded in its names,
> its names embedded in ours.

Un'taneh tókef k'dushat hayom.

We proclaim the powerful sanctity
of this day.

The flush-left English lines in this poem are transliterations, new translations, or adaptations of key lines in the traditional Hebrew text. The
indented lines are wholly new additions, amplifying the meanings of the
traditional prayer.

שופרות

תִּקְעוּ בַחֹדֶשׁ שׁוֹפָר,
בַּכֶּסֶה לְיוֹם חַגֵּנוּ.
—תהלים פא, ד

קוֹל הַשּׁוֹפָר נִשְׁמָע:
הַשָּׁנָה הַחֲדָשָׁה בַּפֶּתַח.

🍂

כָּל־יֹשְׁבֵי תֵבֵל וְשֹׁכְנֵי אָרֶץ:
כִּנְשֹׂא־נֵס הָרִים תִּרְאוּ
וְכִתְקֹעַ שׁוֹפָר תִּשְׁמָעוּ.
—ישעיה יח, ג

קוֹל הַשּׁוֹפָר קוֹרֵא,
מַשְׁקִיט אֶת רוּחֵנוּ,
מֵעִיר בָּנוּ קוֹל דְּמָמָה.

🍂

בְּקָרַחַת הַיַּעַר
שָׁם הַנֶּפֶשׁ פּוֹרַחַת
וְהָעוֹלָם כֻּלּוֹ מֶנֶץ,
שִׁמְעוּ
לַקּוֹל בַּשִּׂיחִים
מֵעֵבֶר לַדֶּשֶׁא.

הַאֲזִינוּ:
הָאִלֵּם מַבִּיעַ אֹמֶר.

(לראש השנה)

Shofarot: Calls

HEARING AND ATTENDING

Sound the shofar on the New Moon,
on our holiday, when the moon is still hidden.
— Psalms 81:4

> The shofar calls, the crescent rises.
> The new year is upon us.

❧

O inhabitants of the world,
you who dwell upon the earth:
When the flag is raised on the mountain — look!
When the shofar is sounded — listen!
–Isaiah 18:3

> The shofar quiets us, wakening us
> to the silence within.

❧

In the clearing, where the mind flowers
and the world sprouts up at every side,
listen
for the sound in the bushes,
behind the grass.

> The shofar takes us into the self
> that is hidden from the self,
> then returns us to the world.
> In the silence we hear the voice of the other,
> we hear what has gone unheard.

(For Rosh Hashanah)

זיכרונות

הַזִּכָּרוֹן מְגַלֶּה לָנוּ
מִי אָנוּ.
הַדִּמְיוֹן לָשׁ אוֹתוֹ
בְּכָל רֶגַע מֵחָדָשׁ.
בְּכָל רֶגַע, הָאֲנִי
לוֹבֵשׁ פָּנִים חֲדָשׁוֹת.

❧

זָכַרְתִּי לָךְ חֶסֶד נְעוּרַיִךְ,
אַהֲבַת כְּלוּלוֹתָיִךְ,
לֶכְתֵּךְ אַחֲרַי בַּמִּדְבָּר,
בְּאֶרֶץ לֹא זְרוּעָה.
—ירמיה ב, ב

מִיַּלְדוּת וְעַד זִקְנָה,
הַקֶּשֶׁר עִם הַזּוּלַת
הוֹלֵךְ וּמַעֲמִיק.

❧

וְזָכַרְתִּי אֲנִי אֶת־בְּרִיתִי אוֹתָךְ
בִּימֵי נְעוּרָיִךְ
וַהֲקִימוֹתִי לָךְ בְּרִית עוֹלָם.
יחזקאל טז, ס—

מִי יִתֵּן וְכָל קְשָׁרֵינוּ
יִהְיוּ כֵּנִים,
הֲדָדִיִּים,
נֶאֱמָנִים.

(לראש השנה)

Zikhronot: Recalling

MEMORY, SELF, AND OTHER

> Recollections shape us, remind us who we are.
> Imagination brings what is buried
> to light.
>
> With each moment recalled,
> the kaleidoscope turns,
> patterns change, colors shift places.
> The selves within the self come into view.

🦋

I remember the lovingkindness of your youthful days,
your love when you were betrothed,
when you followed me in the wilderness,
in the land barren of seed.
— Jeremiah 2:2

> From youth to age,
> our bonds with others deepen,
> become more truthful.

🦋

I will remember my covenant with you
from the days of your youth
and I will establish that covenant for eternity.
— Ezekiel 16:60

> Reciprocity, fidelity:
> the grounding of relationship.

(For Rosh Hashanah)

מלכויות

שְׂאוּ שְׁעָרִים רָאשֵׁיכֶם
וְהִנָּשְׂאוּ פִּתְחֵי עוֹלָם.
—תהלים כד, ז

הַשְּׁעָרִים פְּתוּחִים
לְשִׁפְעַת אֶפְשָׁרֻיּוֹת:
נִשָּׂא עֵינֵינוּ אֲלֵיהֶן.

⊰

לֹא בַשָּׁמַיִם הוּא לֵאמֹר:
מִי יַעֲלֶה־לָּנוּ הַשָּׁמַיְמָה וְיִקָּחֶהָ לָּנוּ, וְיַשְׁמִעֵנוּ אֹתָהּ,
וְנַעֲשֶׂנָּה?

וְלֹא־מֵעֵבֶר לַיָּם הוּא לֵאמֹר:
מִי יַעֲבָר־לָנוּ אֶל־עֵבֶר הַיָּם וְיִקָּחֶהָ לָּנוּ, וְיַשְׁמִעֵנוּ אֹתָהּ,
וְנַעֲשֶׂנָּה?

כִּי־קָרוֹב אֵלֶיךָ הַדָּבָר מְאֹד,
בְּפִיךָ וּבִלְבָבְךָ, לַעֲשֹׂתוֹ.
—דברים ל, יב־יד

נִתְבּוֹנֵן פְּנִימָה.
נְצַפֶּה לְגִלּוּי יְעוּדֵנוּ.

⊰

שְׁמַע, יִשְׂרָאֵל:
הַקְּדֻשָּׁה שׁוֹפַעַת בַּכֹּל,

(לראש השנה)

ENTERING THE GATES

Malkhuyot: Callings

SELF AND ONE

Lift up high, O gates,
lift the eternal portals!
—Psalms 24:7

> The gates are open, portals
> to possibilities:
> What is it that reigns for us supreme?

❧

It is not in the heavens, such that you might say:
Who among us can go up and get it for us and let us hear it
so that we may do it?

And it is not across the sea, such that you might say:
Who will cross the sea for us and get it for us and let us hear it
so that we may do it?

No, it is something very close to you,
in your mouth and in your heart,
for you to do.
—Deuteronomy 30:12–14

> We turn back to ourselves,
> listen for our callings.

❧

Hear, O Israel—

The divine abounds everywhere
and dwells in everything.

(For Rosh Hashanah)

אַלְפֵּי רְבָבָה פָּנֶיהָ,
מְלֹא עוֹלָם שְׁכִינָתָהּ.

הַכֹּל אֶחָד.
—בעקבות דברים ו, ד

Its faces are infinite,
its source suffuses all.

The many are One.
— Adapted from Deuteronomy 6:4

What Do You Have?

Not this earth, not even dust —
Not yours, caw invisible crows
like doors swinging shut.

Not your memories, rising
and burning in the air
like leaf-dew in sun.

Not your thoughts, poking in
and darting out
like hummingbirds among the blossoms.

Only this bit of time (like clouds unforming) —
even as you point to it,
gone.

Nothing

Nothing. You began as nothing and you will end as nothing. And in between — everything, and nothing. In between — joy and sorrow, beauty and decay. Everything yours to partake of, yours to bear. Yours to see, to know, to give birth to — and to let go. None of it yours to have.

Not even you are yours to have. You belong to a wholeness so great you cannot even conceive of it.

No, it is not a belonging; nothing owns you. You are simply part of it. You came out of it and you will return to it. You do not ever leave it, you are part of it forever.

And this is your moment to be alive.

תשובת הלב

אילת השחר שבקע אורה . . .
כך היא גאולתם של ישראל:
בתחילה קמעא־קמעא,
כל מה שהיא הולכת
היא רבה והולכת.
—תלמוד ירושלמי ברכות, א, ה

סִיבּוּב הָאֲדָמָה אִטִּי
אֶל מוּל שָׁמַיִם--

בִּלְתִּי מוּחָשׁ, אַךְ
יוֹצֵר יוֹם וְלַיְלָה.

אֶבֶן אַחַת מֻשְׁלֶכֶת
אֶל תּוֹךְ הַנַּחַל--

וְהַמַּיִם עוֹלִים
קִמְעָה קִמְעָה.

Turning the Heart

[Like] the morning star whose light bursts forth . . .
so Israel's redemption will come:
bit by bit at first,
bigger and bigger as it makes its way.
— Palestinian Talmud Berakhot, 1, 5

Slow spin of earth
against sky —

imperceptible, yet
making the days.

One stone tossed
into the current,

and the river, ever-
so-slightly, rising.

וִדּוּי

עִמְדוּ עַל־דְּרָכִים וּרְאוּ
וְשַׁאֲלוּ לִנְתִבוֹת עוֹלָם
אֵי־זֶה דֶרֶךְ הַטּוֹב, וּלְכוּ־בָהּ
וּמִצְאוּ מַרְגּוֹעַ לְנַפְשְׁכֶם.
—ירמיה ו, טז

בְּמַרְאַת עֵינֵינוּ
מִשְׁתַּקֵּף הַזּוּלַת,

בְּמַרְאַת עֵינֵי הַזּוּלַת
נִגְלִים פָּנֵינוּ.

נַבִּיט פְּנִימָה, נִרְאֶה
אֵיךְ הִכְאַבְנוּ,

אֵיךְ לָן הַכְּאֵב
גַּם בְּפֶצַע קָטָן.

נִשְׁאַל עֲנָוָה
לְבַקֵּשׁ סְלִיחָה,

נִמְצָא מַרְגּוֹעַ
לְנַפְשֵׁנוּ.

(לְיוֹם הַכִּפּוּרִים)

ENTERING THE GATES

Confession

Stand at the roads, and consider.
Look into the paths of the past,
see which is the road of goodness.
Walk it, and find tranquility.
—Jeremiah 6:16

In the mirror of our eyes,
the other is reflected;

in the eyes of the other —
ourselves.

We look outward,
inward,

see how we have hurt
and harmed,

how hurt embeds even
in the smallest wounds.

We give ourselves over,
begin to make amends,

begin
to make ourselves whole.

(For Yom Kippur)
The traditional prayers of confession recited on Yom Kippur are lists,
in abecedarian form, of sins that may have been committed in the past
year by oneself or other members of the community. This re-creation
replaces that catalogue with a call to self-accounting.

אזכור

לזכר נשמות שנגעו בחיי

אַעֲלֶה עַל לִבִּי
אֶת רִקְמַת חַיֶּיהָ/חַיָּיו.

מַרְאוֹת גּוֹאִים
וּנְמוֹגִים,

רְגָעִים
מִתּוֹךְ שֶׁטֶף הַזְּמַן—

עֲנֻגִּים, קָשִׁים,
מַרְנִינִים, פּוֹגְעִים—

לוּ יִהְיוּ נִימֵי הַזִּכְרוֹנוֹת
שְׁזוּרִים בְּמַאֲרַג חַיַּי

לָרֵפֵא.

(ליום הכיפורים)

I Recall

In memory of lives that touched one's own

I call her/him to mind and heart,
the texture of her/his life,
its presence in mine.

Images rise up
and fall away,
moments in the current of time —

tender, harsh,
extraordinary,
mundane,

that which gives pleasure in recollection
and that which hurts, yet resists
being forgotten.

May the threads of memory be woven
into the fabric of my life
and bring healing.

(For Yom Kippur)

כוונות לשעת אבל

הלם. גם כשנדמה שאנו מוכנים, מות יקירינו מגיע אלינו
כהלם. העולם הופך לאחר, וצריך ללמוד, כמו בראשונה,
לחיות.

🍂

הזיכרונות—כמו מבקרים הבאים והולכים בשבעה.
מחזיקים בנו—ומניחים לנו ללכת.

🍂

משהו קטן ויפהפה מופיע, ממלא פיסה של חלל ריק
שנותר, בור בלב שלא נאטם. רגע ראשון, אולי, של
ריפוי.

🍂

אנו דוחים את האפשרות שאבלנו יקטן; אנו חשים שזו
בגידה: כל עוד מתגעגעים אליהם, הם נוכחים. אך החיים
יודעים שהזמן לא ישוב לאחור, שכל הדברים משתנים.
אפילו הצער, אפילו האבל.

🍂

יש נחמה בתחושה שאנו חלק מן העולם—עולם הטבע,
עולם אדם. הבידוד החריף של האבל נכנע לזיכרון יָשָׁן:
איננו לבד.

(ליום הכיפורים)

Passageways of Grieving

Shock. Even when you think you are prepared, it comes as a shock. There was one world before — and another world after. And you must learn, as for the first time, how to live in the world.

❧

They move from room to room, the memories — like visitors entering and leaving the house of *shivah*, where the bereaved sit in mourning. Coming and going, coming and going. Holding on, and letting go.

❧

Something small and beautiful appears, filling part of the vacuum that has been left, the hole in your heart that hasn't closed. The first moment, perhaps, of healing.

❧

You resist believing your grief will diminish, because that belief feels like a betrayal: as long as you go on missing them, they are present. But life carries within itself the knowledge that time will not be undone, that all things change with time. Even your sorrow, even your grief.

❧

The solace of feeling yourself part of the world again — the natural world, the human world. The intense isolation of grief succumbs to an older memory: you are not alone.

(For Yom Kippur)

Service for the High Holidays ❧ 193

ניתן למצוא מרגוע בחופן עפר שהתחמם בשמש, ממש כמו ההבנה שאנו הולכים ומתים מן הרגע בו נולדנו.

התרוממות: הידיעה שאנו חלק מהסוד. הבינה והלב נכנעים: אנו מניחים לעצמנו להילקח.

There comes the knowledge that we are, all of us, always dying. From the moment of birth, dying back into the world, out of which we were born.

A lifting: the awareness that one is part of the mystery. Mind and heart surrender. You let yourself be taken.

תחת כנפי השכינה

כְּנֶשֶׁר יָעִיר קִנּוֹ
עַל־גּוֹזָלָיו יְרַחֵף
יִפְרֹשׂ כְּנָפָיו יִקָּחֵהוּ,
יִשָּׂאֵהוּ עַל־אֶבְרָתוֹ.
דברים לב, יא

הִיא מְרַחֶפֶת מֵעָלֵינוּ—
גּוֹזָלִים נְטוּשִׁים,
שְׁבוּרֵי לֵב—
וְנוֹשֵׂאת אֶת יְגוֹנֵנוּ.

בְּצֵל כְּנָפֶיהָ—
בַּיִת.

(ליום הכיפורים)

Beneath Shekhinah's Wings

Like an eagle stirring its nest,
hovering over its young,
taking them up on widespread wings,
lifting them to its breast.
— Deuteronomy 32:11

She hovers over us,
her fledglings —

the bereaved,
the brokenhearted —

lifts us to her,
takes our sorrow.

In the depth of her shade —
home.

(For Yom Kippur)

Service for the High Holidays   197

תהא

תְּהֵא הַשָּׁנָה הַזֹּאת
טוֹבָה וּמְלֵאָה בְּרָכוֹת:

בִּרְכַּת אַהֲבָה,
בְּרִיאוּת וּגְדִילָה,
דַּעַת וְהַשְׁרָאָה,
וִתּוּר, זֹךְ וָחֶסֶד,
טַעַם וִידִידוּת,

בִּרְכַּת כָּבוֹד,
לִמּוּד, מַזָּל,
נַחַת וְסוֹבְלָנוּת,
עֹנֶג, פַּרְנָסָה, צְדָקָה,
קָרַת רוּחַ וְקִרְבָה,

בִּרְכַּת רַחֲמִים וּרְפוּאָה,
שָׁלוֹם וְשַׁלְוָה,
שָׂשׂוֹן וְשִׂמְחָה,
תִּקְוָה וּתְהִלָּה.

לוּ נִזְכֶּה לְשָׁנָה טוֹבָה.

(לראש השנה)

May It Be So

May the year bring abundant blessings —
beauty, creativity, delight!

May we be confident, courageous,
and devoted to our callings.

May our lives be enriched with education.
May we find enjoyment in our work
and fulfillment in our friendships.

May we grow, may we have good health.
In darker times, may we be sustained
by gratitude and hope.

May we be infused with joy.
May we know intimacy and kindness,
may we love without limit.

May the hours be enhanced with music
and nurtured by art.
May our endeavors be marked by originality.

May we take pleasure in daily living.
May we find peace within ourselves
and help peace emerge in the world.

May we receive the gifts of quiet.

May reason guide our choices,
may romance grace our lives.

May our spirits be serene,
may we find solace in solitude.

(For Rosh Hashanah)

Service for the High Holidays   🌿 199

May we embrace **t**olerance and **t**ruth
and the **u**nderstanding that underlies both.

May we be inspired with **v**ision and **w**onder,
may we be open to e**x**ploration.

May our deepest **y**earnings be fulfilled,
may we be suffused with **z**eal for life.

May we merit these blessings
and may they come to be.
May it be so.

"May It Be So" and its Hebrew counterpart are abecedarian poems,
a type of acrostic in which the initial letters of key words appear in
alphabetical succession. Abecedarians were a popular form of *piyyut*
(liturgical poetry) composed for Rosh Hashanah and Yom Kippur,
typically to delineate sins or to enumerate God's attributes. These new
English and Hebrew abecedarians express wishes, hopes, and blessings.

קדיש: יפעת תבל

הַלְלוּ אֶת הַתֵּבֵל,
הַלְלוּ אֶת מְלוֹאָהּ.

הַלְלוּ אֶת כְּסוּפֶיהָ,
אֶת יָפְיָהּ וִיגוֹנָהּ.

הַלְלוּ אֶבֶן וָאֵשׁ,
נָהָר וְלֵילָךְ

וְצִפּוֹר בּוֹדֵדָה
בַּחַלּוֹן.

הַלְלוּ אֶת רֶגַע
פְּרִיצַת הַשַּׁלֵם

וְאֶת רֶגַע פְּרִיצַת
הַשָּׁלֵם בְּרִנָּה.

הַלְלוּ בְּכָל מְאוֹדְכֶם
אֶת הַיֹּפִי הַדּוֹעֵךְ — וּרְאוּ

כִּי יִפְעַת הַתֵּבֵל
הִיא לָכֶם.

Kaddish: Beauty of the World

Praise the world —
praise its fullness

and its longing,
its beauty and its grief.

Praise stone and fire,
lilac and river,

and the solitary bird
at the window.

Praise the moment
when the whole
bursts through pain

and the moment
when the whole
bursts forth in joy.

Praise the dying beauty
with all your breath,
and praising, see

the beauty of the world
is your own.

Five ❦ Re-visioning
Un'taneh Tókef K'dushat Hayom

על "ונתנה תוקף קדושת היום"

Structure, Content, and Theology: An Overview

"Judge, Prosecutor, Expert, and Witness, the One Who inscribes and seals and does the accounting" — so God is portrayed in the opening paragraph of *"Un'taneh Tôkef K'dushat Hayom*: We Declare the Utter Sanctity of this Day," a *piyyut* (liturgical poem) in the Ashkenazic rite that has come to embody the central themes and images of the High Holidays.* When the great shofar is sounded, we are told, even the angels are "seized by fear and trembling," knowing that no one is presumed innocent in God's sight. On the Day of Judgment, all the world's creatures will stand before God "like a flock of sheep" herded beneath the staff of their shepherd, waiting to be counted and appraised. The final verdict — the "decree" — will spell life or death.

God's absolute sovereignty over all creation and His power to determine all destinies are encapsulated in the line that has become iconic of the Days of Awe: "On Rosh Hashanah it is written and on Yom Kippur it is sealed."† The reference is to the "book of life," in which God inscribes our fates for the new year. This pronouncement introduces a catalogue of pairings that constitute what may be the most fearsome lines in the Rosh Hashanah and Yom Kippur liturgies:

How many will leave this life
and how many will be born into it,

Un'taneh Tôkef was originally written for Rosh Hashanah (in the Byzantine period, in the land of Israel) and subsequently became part of the Yom Kippur liturgy as well.

†References to God as personified or gendered reflect the language and theology of the texts being quoted or paraphrased.

who will live and who will die,
whose life will reach its natural end
and whose will be cut short . . .

The list goes on, enumerating in stark pairs of opposites the benign and dreadful possibilities awaiting us. At its conclusion, however, the emphasis shifts. We are told that we can affect God's judgments of us by means of *t'shuvah* (repentance or, as I render it, "returning"), *t'filah* (prayer), and *tz'dakah* (charity or good deeds). I will say more about these key words shortly.

Having acknowledged our sins and the need to atone, *Un'taneh Tókef* now addresses God directly, pleading for mercy and compassion, reminding Him that we are His own creation, mere "flesh and blood," and praising the side of His nature that is "slow to anger and inclined to be appeased."

Then comes a dramatic turn: we leave the severe world of judgment and enter an elegiac realm. An assembly of biblical verses describes, in a cascade of increasingly poignant metaphors, the fragility and transient nature of life. This brief, lyrical passage is one of the most moving parts of the liturgy.

The tone shifts yet again in the *piyyut*'s last section, which is at once evocative and enigmatic. After contrasting our mortality with God's eternal being, *Un'taneh Tókef* affirms, "You have called our name by [or according to] Yours." This assertion may be meant to be comforting, an antidote to the fear and awe that have by now overtaken us; or it may be intended to remind God of His bond with us, so that He will treat us favorably when the time comes to pronounce judgment. Perhaps both interpretations apply.

But what exactly does it mean, the linking of our name with God's? *Un'taneh Tókef* leaves this and many other questions open.

It also leaves us with a theology that has challenged commentators for centuries. The idea that reward and punishment follow causally from our actions is, on the face of it, neither credible nor helpful in the search for life's meaning. Nor is the image of God as judge a useful companion in that search. Yet attempts to soften the theological stance of *Un'taneh Tókef* by downplaying its inherent determinism and emphasizing our part in influencing God's decisions leave the dilemma intact: Why are so many good people struck down and so many bad people allowed to thrive? Indeed, the suggestion that we have power over our ultimate destinies only highlights the contradiction between the fairness that the *piyyut* seems to promise and the reality we face every day.

Rabbis and other thinkers have taken steps to interpret *Un'taneh Tókef* more meaningfully for modern readers and worshipers.* I put forth my own approach here, to contribute to the conversation and to explain why and how I recreated this *piyyut*.

---

*See, for example, some of the essays in Lawrence Hoffman, ed., *Who by Fire, Who by Water*, 2010. Joel Hoffman's entry, "How Was Your Flight?" (93–97), argues that the inclusion of images derived from the Book of Job demonstrates that the author of the *piyyut* is aware that sin is not the direct cause of all suffering. See also Marc Saperstein, "Inscribed for Life or Death?," *Journal of Reform Judaism* 28, 1981:18–26.

The View from Within

If we allow that the theme of judgment is the "frame" of *Un'taneh Tókef,* what might we see when we lift off the frame and look at the unembellished picture? We find it is the bold face of death that gazes back at us. My re-creation focuses on this confrontation, which is at the heart of the *piyyut*'s power.

The traditional *Un'taneh Tókef* is made up of multiple segments, as sketched above. We might think of these as movements, analogous to those of a musical composition. The re-creation structures the *piyyut* in four such movements.

The first of these opens with Hebrew lines taken from the original:

Un'taneh tókef k'dushat hayom
ki hu nora v'ayom.

Uv'shofar gadol yitaka
v'kol d'mamah dakah yishama.

We declare the utter sanctity of this day
for it is an awe-filled day.

A great shofar is sounded
and a voice of slender silence is heard.

"A voice of slender silence" is my rendering of the oft-quoted biblical phrase *kol d'mamah dakah* (1 Kings 19:12), which has been translated in various ways but is best known to English readers as it appears in the King James Version of 1611: "a still small voice." This wording has been adopted in many of the standard Hebrew-English prayer books from the major movements of Judaism; other translations in the prayer books include "a still, thin sound" and "a small quiet voice."*

Despite differences in nuance, almost all versions of this phrase are based on a reversal of the original Hebrew syntax. That is, the Hebrew does not describe a voice that is still (or quiet) and small (or thin). Rather, it speaks of a silence that is *itself* thin — an image even more elusive than the one we are accustomed to.

I try to capture the evocativeness of this paradoxical image by means of poetic expansion, or amplification. The stanza below suggests that the voice of silence comes not from without but from within. Yet the "within" need not be isolated; we are, each of us, part of the human chorus and the greater whole of the natural world.

> The voice is one's own —
> a reed in the chorus,
> a breath in the wind.

*Versions of the prayer book giving "a/the still small voice" include: Morris Silverman, *High Holiday Prayer Book*, 1951 (Conservative); Edward Feld, *Mahzor Lev Shalem*, 2010 (Conservative); Jules Harlow, *A Prayer Book for the Days of Awe*, 1972 (Conservative); Jonathan Sacks, *The Koren Rosh Hashanah Mahzor*, 2011 (Orthodox); Chaim Stern, *Gates of Repentance*, 1978 (Reform). Other translations from standard prayer books include: "a gentle whisper," Philip Birnbaum, *High Holyday Prayer Book*, 1951 (Orthodox); "a still, thin sound," Nosson Scherman, *The Complete Art Scroll Mahzor*, 1985 (Orthodox); "a small quiet voice," David Teutsch, *Kol Haneshamah*, 1999 (Reconstructionist). Many more variants can be found among Bible translations, including: "a soft, murmuring sound," Jewish Publication Society (1985, 1999); "a low murmuring sound," New English Bible (1970); "a sound of sheer silence," New Revised Standard Version (1989). Joel Hoffman proposes "a thin whisper of a sound" (L. Hoffman, 29).

The second movement of the new *Un'taneh Tókef* also begins with Hebrew lines from the original:

B'rosh hashanah yikateyvun
uv'yom tzom kipur yeyḥateymun.

On Rosh Hashanah it is written
and on Yom Kippur it is sealed.

The metaphor of inscription is then amplified:

Our lives are stories
inscribed in time.

At the turning of the year
we look back, look ahead, see

that we are always
in the days between

What follows is the most raw and vivid passage in the *piyyut*. The re-creation presents the original passage in its entirety, without modification, not only because it gives us a picture of a much earlier period in our history, but because, despite some of its archaic details, it still grips us today:

How many will leave this life
and how many will be born into it,
who will live and who will die,
whose life will reach its natural end
and whose will be cut short,
who by water and who by fire,
who by sword and who by beast,
who by hunger and who by thirst,
who by quake and who by plague,
who by choking and who by stoning,

who will rest and who will wander,
who will be tranquil and who will be torn,
who will be at peace and who will be tormented,
who will be raised high and who will be brought low,
who will prosper and who will be impoverished.

The third movement focuses on the *piyyut*'s central assertion: *ut'shuvah ut'filah utz'dakah ma'avirin et-ró'a hag'zerah*, commonly understood as "and/but repentance and prayer and charity [or good deeds] avert the evil decree."* No two prayer books of the main Jewish denominations render this line in exactly the same way — a testament to the challenges it poses to interpretation.† To plumb the meanings of the line, it bears our looking closely at each of its components.

---

*In Hebrew, the conjunction "and" attaches to the word following it. Thus *ut'shuvah* means "and *t'shuvah*," *ut'filah* means "and *t'filah*," *utz'dakah* means "and *tz'dakah*."

†Following are the English translations as they appear in the Orthodox, Conservative, Reform, and Reconstructionist prayer books: "But repentance, prayer, and charity cancel the stern decree," Orthodox, Philip Birnbaum, *High Holyday Prayer Book* (1951); "But repentance, prayer, and charity remove the evil of the decree!" Orthodox, Nosson Scherman, *The Complete Art Scroll Mahzor* (1985); "But repentance, prayer and righeousness avert the severe decree," Conservative, Morris Silverman, *High Holiday Prayer Book* (1951); "But T'shuvah, T'fillah, and Tz'dakah have the power to transform the harshness of the decree," Conservative, Edward Feld, *Mahzor Lev Shalem* (2010); "But penitence, prayer and good deeds can annul the severity of the decree," Conservative, Jules Harlow, *A Prayer Book for the Days of Awe* (1972); "But repentance, prayer, and charity temper judgment's severe decree," Reform, Chaim Stern, *Gates of Repentance* (1978); "But teshuvah, and tefilah, and tzedakah make easier what God may decree," Reconstructionist, David Teutsch, *Kol Haneshamah* (1999). Joel Hoffman proposes "And repentance, prayer, and charity / Help the hardship of the decree pass" (L. Hoffman, 13).

The View from Within

The three nouns that make up the line's compound subject signify three key concepts in the High Holiday liturgy. The first of these is *t'shuvah*, translated variously in the prayer books as "repentance," "penitence," and "Teshuvah." "Repentance" and "penitence" are similarly misleading: both derive from the Latin *paenitire*, meaning "to be sorry" (the word "penitentiary," a place of punishment, is etymologically related). But *paenitire* is a far cry from the Hebrew word-root of *t'shuvah—shuv*, meaning "to return" or "to do again." The rendering of *t'shuvah* as "Teshuvah" is, of course, a surrender to the impossibility of translation. I suggest instead "turning (inward)" and "returning (to one's self)" as the equivalents of *t'shuvah* in this context.

The second noun in the subject is *t'filah*. Although at first glance "prayer" would seem to be an adequate translation of this word, what constitutes prayer for people today is by no means obvious. To take into account the multiple sensibilities of both theists and nontheists, the idea of contemplation might meaningfully be brought in. "Contemplation," from the Latin *templum*: temple, an open or consecrated space, a place for observation.

Tz'dakah, the third noun in the chain, also demands more than a single word to represent it in English. Usually translated as "charity," *tz'dakah* contains within it the root *tz-d-k*, "justice." Thus, embedded in *tz'dakah* is the central Jewish teaching that giving to those in need is not just an act of goodwill but also a moral mandate.

The compound subject *ut'shuvah ut'filah utz'dakah* is followed by the verb *ma'avirin*, which derives from the Hebrew root meaning "pass" or "cross over." Some of the standard translations of *ma'avirin*, including "cancel," "avert," and "annul," connote actions that are much more emphatic than those implied by the Hebrew.* Other translations, such as "temper" and "make easier," are closer to the mark.

The crux of the interpretation — the point at which the line can pivot in radically different ways — comes with the object of the verb, *ró'a hag'zerah*, commonly rendered in English as "the evil decree," "the severe decree," or "the stern decree" ("decree" being understood as the sentence of life or death). Each of these various translations is, however, misleading: *ró'a hag'zerah* is not "the evil [or severe, or stern] decree" but rather "the evil [or the severity, or sternness] *of* the decree" — a seemingly small but important distinction. The statement that *t'shuvah*, *t'filah*, and *tz'dakah* nullify "the evil decree" suggests that righteousness ensures one a positive fate and even provides a stay against death — a suspect, if not absurd, assertion. If, however, we speak about these virtues as tempering "the evil *of* the decree," we are saying something quite different. We are not maintaining that *ró'a* ("evil") characterizes the decree itself but, rather, that it represents some *aspect* or *component of* the decree. It becomes our task to interpret what that aspect might be.

While there are modern translations that render the syntax of *ró'a hag'zerah* accurately,† most do not follow the consequences of this rendering far enough. I suggest we think about *ró'a hag'zerah* as our difficulty in confronting the decree — confronting what *will*, sooner or later, come

*Saperstein points out that in the midrashic source of this passage the verb is *m'vat'lin* (cancel or annul). I agree with his assertion that the verb that appears in the liturgical version, *ma'avirin*, gives a significantly different meaning to the line.

†See, for example, some of the prayer books previously cited and some of the essays in L. Hoffman.

to pass. The difficulty is compounded, of course, because it is not just our own death we must face: contemplating the deaths of those we love can be even more painful than anticipating our own end. Yet preparing oneself for these inevitabilities is an essential challenge of a well-lived life. If we look at *ut'shuvah ut'filah utz'dakah ma'avirin et-ró'a hag'zerah* with greater openness to its potential, we may find it offers meaningful guidance for this greatest of all tasks.*

My re-creation divides the line *ut'shuvah ut'filah utz'dakah ma'avirin et-ró'a hag'zerah* into four elements. In the English version of the re-creation, each element is rendered with a longer phrase, filling in connotations that would be lost in a word-for-word translation. Thus *t'shuvah* here is a turning toward the self, *t'filah* includes outer-directed prayer as well as inwardly focused contemplation, and *tz'dakah* implies both charity and moral obligation.

Ut'shuvah
Turning inward
to face one's self

Ut'filah
Entering into prayer
and contemplation

Utz'dakah
Giving to the needy,
as justice requires

---

*Saperstein goes in a different direction, referring to the "evil potential" of the decree, which inheres in the way we respond to suffering or loss.

Ma'avirin et-ró'a hag'zerah
These diminish the harshness
of the decree

The four elements are then amplified (in the English
and in the Hebrew):

Ut'shuvah
> Returning to the inner artistry
> that gives each life its form,
>
> seeking to become
> one's truest self

Ut'filah
> Being alive to the unending flow
> within and around us,
>
> holding dear
> the transient beauty

Utz'dakah
> Knowing that we are, all of us,
> flesh and blood
>
> and our fates are intertwined—
> sweet with bitter, bitter with salt—
>
> and that the fruit of kindness
> is kindness,
>
> and good deeds
> are its fulfillment

Ma'avirin et-ró'a hag'zerah
> We become present
> to the fullness of our lives

and untether ourselves from the fear
of what lies ahead.

The fourth movement of the re-creation presents the elegiac montage of biblical verses as it appears in the traditional *piyyut*, with one modification: where the original refers to "man" and "he," the re-creation says "we."

> We begin in earth
> and we end in earth.
> We spend our lives earning our bread.
> We are like broken vessels,
> dry grass, withering blossoms,
> passing shadows, vanishing clouds,
> drifting wind, scattering dust,
> a fleeting dream.

Three lines of amplification extend the portrayal of mortality:

> Born in nature
> and borne by nature,
> we die in its lap-and-fold.

The next stanzas re-vision the final section of the original *piyyut*, which highlights the contrast between our mortality and God's eternality. The new lines include an interpretation of the statement "You have called our name by Yours." If our names are our unique identities — our "selves" — the linking of our names with God's suggests that we participate in something larger than our individual selves. The deeper truth of our identities is that we are all part of a great oneness.

The whole lives on,
infinite in mystery,
its manifestations numberless.

Looking beyond our separate deaths,
we find our selves in the greater whole,
our names embedded in its names,
its names embedded in ours.

As individuals we die, each of us, without exception. But the whole of life does not perish. When we are able to see beyond our separateness and feel our enduring connection to that whole, we find a deeper sense of self. Death, too, accrues new meaning.

Nothing—no words, no poetry however eloquent—can fully extinguish the pain we feel in grappling with the inevitability of suffering and death. But living one's life with integrity (*t'shuvah*) and with thoughtful appreciation (*t'filah*) and with acceptance of one's responsibility for others (*tz'dakah*) can ease the difficulty and diminish the hardship (*ma'avirin et-róa hag'zerah*).

The re-creation closes with a reprise of the opening, translated afresh:

Un'taneh tókef k'dushat hayom.

We proclaim the powerful sanctity
of this day.

Acknowledgments

I am grateful to the Hadassah-Brandeis Institute for its generosity to me over the years, and for grants in 2005, 2006, and 2007 to enable the writing of this book. In particular, I thank the institute's co-director, Shula Reinharz, and its administrator, Deborah Olins, for their kindness.

My deep gratitude goes to Nancy Augustus for encouragement and support of every kind. Nancy prompted and prodded until the book was launched in me, and she sustained me throughout its creation. It would not have happened without her.

I benefited greatly from Snira Klein's sensitivity to the nuances of Hebrew when I began composing the blessings in this book. Stephen Damon inspired me during the project's initial stages and later moved it forward with probing questions and provocative suggestions. Deborah Enelow's responses to the book's structure and content were always keenly insightful. Richard Sarason shared his expert knowledge of liturgy and rabbinics, providing a wealth of historical and critical background.

I am fortunate in having yet more colleagues and friends who contributed their expertise. I thank Nancy Andell, Hamutal Bar-Yosef, Hava Pinhas Cohen, Lucille Day, Hillel Furstenberg, Rochelle Furstenberg, David Harband, Naamah Kelman, Scott-Martin Kosofsky, Dalia Marx, Judith Plaskow, Valerie Zakovitch, Shai Zarchi, and Sheva Zucker.

Beth Lieberman faithfully guided the book toward publication, and Bonny Fetterman was a terrific author's representative. Bronwyn Becker shepherded the book gracefully and wisely throughout its production. In addition to providing early suggestions for shaping the project, Suzanne Singer helped the book reach its rabbinical audience, as did Sylvia Fuks Fried, governor of Brandeis University Press. Phyllis Deutsch, editor-in-chief of the University Press of

New England, was the book's enthusiastic champion. As a Brandeis alumna, I am especially pleased to have Brandeis as my publisher.

The Lenore Bohm-Leichtag Family Foundation contributed financially to the project, as did Nancy Augustus, Barbara Frame, Nan Fink Gefen, Laura Geller, Victoria Hertz, J. Hannah Kranzberg, Suzanne Singer, Judy Chasnoff Smith, Marion Sondermann, and Jan and Peter Tras. I am extremely appreciative of their generosity.

The drawing on the cover, "Gilead Apples," was made at Gilead Tree Farm, home of my dear friends Lillian and Paul Steinfeld. Their spirit, along with that of their daughter, Beth, of blessed memory, infuses these pages.

And two people without whom I could not have brought the project to fruition:

Yair Zakovitch, Bible scholar, Hebrew poet, and friend of many years, reviewed the Hebrew portions of the book and worked with me for long days, polishing blessings and translating my English poems into Hebrew. Yair brought to the project an immeasurable trove of knowledge and literary acumen; the richness he added cannot be overstated.

Steve Rood, finest of poets and ever my best reader, viewed draft upon draft of the English—poems and prose, introductions and footnotes, commas and line breaks—until his eyes were bleary and the book was closed for the night. "Let's give it a morning look," he'd say—and in the morning we'd start up again, picking over words. Alas, there aren't enough words to convey how much better Steve has made all my work.

HBI Series on Jewish Women

Shulamit Reinharz, *General Editor*
Sylvia Barack Fishman, *Associate Editor*

The HBI Series on Jewish Women, created by the Hadassah-Brandeis Institute, publishes a wide range of books by and about Jewish women in diverse contexts and time periods. Of interest to scholars and the educated public, the HBI Series on Jewish Women fills major gaps in Jewish Studies and in Women and Gender Studies as well as their intersection.

The HBI Series on Jewish Women is supported by a generous gift from Dr. Laura S. Schor.

Marcia Falk's acclaimed translation, *The Song of Songs: Love Lyrics from the Bible*, was published in the HBI series in 2004. *The Days Between: Blessings, Poems, and Directions of the Heart for the Jewish High Holiday Season* is the long-awaited successor to *The Book of Blessings*, her re-creation of Jewish prayer from a nonhierarchical, inclusive perspective.

For the complete list of books that are available in this series, please see www.upne.com.